Praise

BIG ROOLZ

"Though but pale light doth yon scribe impart upon the deep, light it yet be still." – W. Shakespeare

"I'm not the least bit jealous. Shut up." – S. Freud

"WTF is this shit?" – Abraham Lincoln

"I cannot be but thoroughly diverted by the splendid and inventive wordplay of this fine sir." – Jane Austen

"My name is Ozymandias, king of kings; Look on Berit's works, ye Mighty, and despair!" – The Oz Man

"That bastard Berit is a pussy but he beat me at poker so here's a fucking quote, a quote to pay the bill, the debt of a drunken card game at 3 AM in a dark smoky room littered with bottles and cigar butts and the despair of old drunk men with no place else to be." – E. Hemingway

"I have no idea what this is but I kinda dig it." – Caesar Augustus

"A way more worthwhile read than The Republic." – Socrates

"Socrates can suck my quill." – Plato

"Well, shit. Now there are only eight circles in Hell." – Dante Alighieri

"I merely gave an ear to my love. Berit gives his entire heart to his readers. Which isn't saying much." – Vinny Van Gogh

"I wept when there was no more book to read." – Great, Alexander the

THE LITTLE BOOK OF BIG ROOLZ

BOOK 1

SK BERIT

Copyright © 2018 SK Berit, LLC. All rights reserved.
The author and publisher have provided this book, in whatever-the-fuck form you got it, for your own stupid personal use. Making it public in any way is bad manners, mean, and against the goddamn law. Doesn't matter what shitty country you live in. If you fuck with the author's rights, you shall be dealt with immediately, and without the least bit of ruth. I know a guy in Brazil who handles these jobs for less money than you can imagine. You've been fucking warned.

ISBN: 9781729170441

Cover design: Louise Thomas
Barney the Owl Copyright © 2018 Louise Thomas, used with permission
Additional art: SK Berit

Dedication

To the people who never give up on themselves. May you find a little bit of fuel in these pages to help you keep going.

Acknowledgments

Huge multicolor fireworks of thanks to the wonderful people of my two tiny little Facebook groups. You make me smile every day.

The support of family has never wavered, even when it could have.

Mr. Kelly, Mr. Butler, Miss Fritz (I'm still upset that you got married). One day you might get an idea of the profound influence you had on this scrawny doofus, back when I was a scrawny doofus. I have managed to stop being scrawny, at least.

Pegs. You stood by me and with me through some rough times without flinching.

Thank you, all of you. Each of you. I could not have done this without the efforts and support of every one of you. If I failed to tell you how much it has meant to me, please accept this as a small portion of recompense.

Then there's this.

Nearly every author and writer must spend time at a day job while we chisel away at our word sculptures. The hope of eventually supporting ourselves from the publication of our efforts is often never realized but one thing above all else drives us ever onward.

Shitty bosses.

It is high time the writing community acknowledges the immense debt owed to the pricks, bitches, and assholes that provide daily motivation to writers the world over to keep chipping away and hoping for the day we can tell our imbecilic overlords to fuck off.

The worst part is every shitty boss thinks I'm talking about somebody else. No, idiot, I'm pointing my middle finger at you (Gary), and raising a glass with the other hand.

Here's to the shitty bosses who supply the creative world with 82.371% of our motivation to keep going.

Foreword

When I look at someone, I try to look at what is amazing about them. Watching through the eyes of magic, I silently observe their wildness and their magnificence so that I may see them as they are, not as the world expects me to see them. This is what happened when I took a closer look at SK Berit and the world that orbits him.

It was an average day when I received the draft version of The Little Book of Big Roolz. It wasn't dressed fancy at all; in fact, I believe the draft was still wearing its pajamas. I opened it between other tasks for a quick flick through and then I got lost. When I laughed out loud a few times, I drew curious looks from others. My bestie even rolled her chair over to my desk to get in on the action.

What started out as a scan, quickly became a very focused operation that involved conspiratorial giggles behind our hands and quick glances over our shoulders for any sightings of the imagined fun police. When there was no sign of morbid authority, we climbed in even deeper until we were up to our necks in it. Eventually we each only had one eye sticking out of the time pocket, keeping watch.

In the interactions that I've had with the author, I have come to know a man of quick wit and deep thought who has a zero-tolerance policy for nonsense. He has deep knowledge of himself and the world, unrestricted humor, and is free of so many of the chains that restrict and restrain the rest of us. He is a thinker, an observer and a fighter who, I believe, has had his steel tested more times than he would let anyone know.

I have learned that not being able to walk in the shoes of another does not stop us from hearing and absorbing the music that comes from the chords they strike with their actions. To know someone, we need only know what delights and revolts them, and how hard they will fight to become the fire that burns against the cold.

To trust someone, we need only know what they are capable of when they have enormous influence. To respect someone, we need only know that they hold us in high regard too. SK Berit is the kind of man who follows his soul because he knows it knows the way. I admire him for this.

We are so often convinced by our societies to be rigid in our thinking, to obey, not push back, not question and not stand out. We admire labels over courage, position over principle, and material wealth over truthfulness. We say one thing and do another without even realizing our own contradictions. We live in dread, trapped by moral and social contracts that we hate and judge, yet we cling to them with white knuckles and pained faces, expecting others to also toe the line. SK is no such sheep. He walks a wide berth around the pinched and appropriate, sewing wild flowers in the concrete, knowing they will bring about the next revolution and set the rest of mankind free.

Through hurt we either break or grow, through loss we either cling too hard or we learn the value in setting stuff free. It's through fear that we either fight back or grovel at the feet of our undeserving lords. SK Berit is a man who has rebelled and fought back and because of it, has won.

We do not need to be able to see the monster to know that it's there, but slaying the monster is done one page at a time. *The Little Book of Big Roolz* rips a thousand different strips off every kind of beast that we've been taught to fear.

This book will not allow you to remain locked in a contradiction between your dreams and the dead bureaucracies and vain façades of our species. It will bring back the sweetness that is lost in the silence of your paradox. At every turn it will no longer allow you to suppress and restrain your excitement, hunger and joy. It will take you by the heart and guide you away from distraction, cynicism and dysfunctional medication.

The warriors, like SK, who come through the fields and bastions of hardship, piece themselves back together, one shattered sliver at a time, and eventually break free and make a difference. They build their own opinions and define their own principles and values, chasing a purpose, they become the knights who set the rest of us free from our self-imposed restraints.

This book is about the rules that we haven't managed to figure out for ourselves. It is written in plain language, wearing lipstick in all the places you would never think to look.

Knights show us the difference between giving up and knowing when we've lost. Most of us just give up before we even start. May the rules in this book teach you how to stand in your own sun again.

May it encourage those who devour it. Courage, as you know, is a lot like gravity, all it takes is a little push.

SK conducts himself with abundant levity and is the shimmering sword in the darkness.

This book is a bursting ray of sunshine mixed with a little tornado. I just love it.

Angela Shearer
Author of *Relevant*

Introduction

> *When the pupil is ready the Master will appear.* – Some Lying Sack of Shit

Holy shit! You're reading my book!

Holy shit! I have a book for you to read!

I have to say, writing a book is something I have always wanted to *have done*. The actual doing of it has been like doing a really, really hard thing. Like sooper hard. More harder, even, than say, writing a paper in college, if you can believe it. No, I mean it!

Like, you know, totally hard to do.

And here it is, and here you are reading it. I'm absolutely the kind of guy who would read over your shoulder then wait for your reaction to my favorite parts. *Wait, nothing? At all? My world makes no sense anymore. Where's the rope? No, it isn't for me. You're the one who didn't get the joke.*

This is where I am supposed to give you the deeply meaningful, perhaps circuitous but still serendipitous, route that led me to be typing these words for the opening of my books.

Let's count that as your first disappointment. There will be others, I promise you. But a least we got it out of the way early. Yay!

Let me make something abundantly clear up front: I don't want to be writing this book.

I would so much more prefer to buy it and read it.

Problem is, nobody has written it yet. Bastards.

Pieces of it, yes, here or there. I don't claim to be the original thinker on most of the shit I write about. Some of it is original to me, but largely I have collated bits of knowledge and wisdom gleaned from others and pasted it together in a different way.

Let me be clear about another point.

I'm not a scientist. I'm not a researcher. I'm not a therapist. If you think academic credentials are a deal-breaker, then you might as well close this book and move on down the (actual or virtual) aisle until you can find an author with some alphabet soup after their name.

I'm just a guy who needed this shit as much, or more, than you do. The only difference is I went looking for it.

Before you jump onto social media with some form of "Who the fuck does this guy think he is?" let me just say I'm waaay ahead of you, pal. I've been thinking the same thing for decades.

Here is the short answer: I'm nobody.

Happy yet? Didn't think so. Dumbass.

If you look at the externalities of my life there is no fucking reason why I should be the one writing this book, and certainly no reason why you should be reading it.

And yet, here we are.

For some reason, the specific combination of genetics, environment, and experience that landed on me has allowed me to think, question, and understand some aspects of our existence in ways that haven't been previously identified. I'm damn good at finding connections in disparate phenomena.

Jesus, what a load of big-assed words.

What I mean to say is that shit happens to me, and I try to understand it. I collect bits of knowledge like a taxidermist collects dead animals. These bits float around in my head until they collide with other bits, and occasionally that creates a pretty little spark.

I don't know why this has happened/fallen to me. I didn't ask for it or want it.

One day, I was considering the quote at the top. I was seriously wondering where the hell my master was. But then, it came to me.

Somebody will be the first master.

Once upon a time, nobody knew how to knap arrowheads out of flint. Then some guy tried a bunch of shit until he found what worked best. That was improved upon by lots of other guys over eons. Eventually, some of them became the first masters at making arrowheads.

I cannot express loudly enough how much I do not want to be anyone's master. It would be better for everyone if this book came from some highbrow intellectual with decades of science and research behind him/her/it. I just want to read a book like this. I do not want to write it.

At some point while reading this book you may come to hate me for what I wrote or how I wrote it or what you think I meant when I wrote it.

It's not an actual objective of mine, so you know. It is an artifact of my style, and because I am fairly-ish committed to speaking plainly. Also, I am a sarcastic smartass. For some people (even within my genetic family) that is a deal-breaker.

I write with a tone and style that isn't necessarily how I feel. Can you even imagine? Somebody adopting a persona on the page that isn't how they are in real life? The horror!

Sometimes I write words that do not even reflect my own beliefs on a topic, but I write them to get the reader to think. I provoke, on occasion, just to get you to react, to get you out of your big, comfy, coffin-shaped bubble.

[*Shut up! Bubbles can be coffin shaped!* – SK]

Lots of people should not be reading this book. Here is a partial list. People who…

…need/expect/demand Trigger Warnings. Here's the only warning I will offer: run away now. No, even farther. Keep going until you find yourself in a tub of cotton candy. Then eat yourself into a hyperglycemic coma surrounded by elves and good fairies and only nice words. Fucking pansies.

…are looking for confirmation of their life choices. You are so screwed if you keep reading.

…expect some fucking dry-as-cowshit-in-the-desert examination of the topics. Pretty sure this bullet point settles that point rather thoroughly.

…are so deeply wedded to their assumptions that they cannot imagine any other meaning to the use of words than their own. Meh, these folks are gone already.

…have undergone even a partial humor-ectomy. How have you managed to read this far without rolling your eyes in disgust? I'm a teeny bit impressed. I warn you, however, it will not get easier for you going forward.

…cringe at profanity. They would rather continue in their pursuit of ignorance than feel a tad uncomfortable at naughty words. Which they think in their minds but believe not speaking them gives them some sort of moral edge. It does not. Sorry.

...only read books like this to find fault.

Let me save you a whole bunch of trouble. This entire book is fraught with problems and faults, and flaws and inconsistencies because guess what? It was written by a human being. I fuck up all the time. My ideas today will be embarrassing to me before long. That's how this shit works, and it works pretty fucking well. Take your righteous indignation somewhere else.

Oh, and sometimes I employ phrasing designed more to be humorous than strictly accurate. It's called trying to be funny. I'm sure you've heard of it. Or read about it.

The good news for the rest of you: the people above have already self-selected out of this volume, so we can continue unmolested. Woohoo!

For the three of you still reading, allow me a small suggestion as you proceed. Let go of your assumptions about what I mean. You have your own meanings for everything. Allow that my own might, just maybe, differ from yours, and that you cannot know my meanings if you assign your own to mine.

Oh shit, that was deep and heavy, man.

Very simply, let me have my own meanings for the words and phrases I use. Allow that they might be different from your meanings. We can both hold different meanings and it's OK if we don't impose our meanings on each other.

I only ask one thing: please try to be pragmatic. Either this shit works, it makes sense and helps you understand people (your call if that includes you) a little bit better, or it doesn't. Nothing else matters. The question of if "it works" is in your own hands. You find out by doing the shit I talk about. Sure, you can judge it on an intellectual level, but that's for pussies who are afraid of the world.

You can argue if research supports my positions or not. I don't care. It has no impact on the efficacy of what I say. I live in the actual world, not in some fucking laboratory. That's no dig at the lab rats who have done so much to make our world better. It's a dig at the insecure little shits who need guarantees before they will wiggle a toe.

If you have any guts at all, put my words to the test, and find out for yourself. Sadly, most of you do not have such courage. It may sound passive-aggressive, but that's just the facts. If you happen to be weak minded enough to respond to such tactics, I won't complain. Out loud. For now.

Enough of this shit. It's time to jump in.

Preamble

You just want the fucking book to get *started* but you're so damn anal about reading every precious word that you won't skip even this worthless section I put in just to fuck with you.

Seriously, this is completely void of meaning, or context, or anything remotely helpful. It's just filler. But at least it has the courage to admit to being filler.

If that, in fact, requires courage. I'm not entirely convinced that it does. And by 'not entirely' I mean, not even a little bit.

Suckers.

Part I: Everything You Know is Wrong

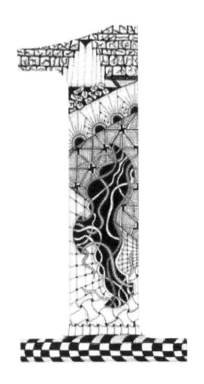

Who Are You?

It is better to be hated for what you are than to be loved for what you are not. – André Gide

You are going to read a lot of shit in this book, and some of it will seem harsh. I do that on purpose. But first, there is something very near to my heart to discuss absent any snark.

I want to say the first thing to do if you want a better/different life is to decide to have it. But that's not accurate for most people.

Sure, if you have a very sturdy sense of self, then yeah, go ahead and jump ahead to the deciding part. This is for the rest of the world, the ones who haven't lived as themselves yet. You who have parked your true self so deeply underground you can't even know for sure if it exists. You think you are the only person like this, but you are not.

You are one among multitudes.

I found out by accident when on a whim, I read this from Alice Miller's outstanding book, *The Drama of the Gifted Child* [emphasis mine].

Accommodation to parental needs often (but not always) leads to the "as-if personality." This person develops in such a way that he reveals only what is expected of him and fuses so completely with what he reveals that one could scarcely guess how much more there is to him behind this false self. He cannot develop and differentiate his true self, because he is unable to live it. Understandably, this person will complain of a sense of emptiness, futility, or homelessness, *for the emptiness is real.* A process of emptying, impoverishment, and crippling of his potential actually took place. The integrity of the child was injured when all that was alive and spontaneous in him was cut off.

The impact of this paragraph on my life was absolute. It devastated every lie, every facade, every pretense that had been place upon me and that I had both accepted and fought against. You know what I mean, I know you do.

Be the good child. Don't rock the boat. Follow the rules. Don't step out of line. Go to this college, study that subject. Play sports. Never play sports. Whatever it was that people laid on you that wasn't what you wanted, that kept you from experiencing your true self, this is where everything begins.

Your liberation, I mean.

Chances are nobody has spoken to you of this before. It might break you wide open. That's what happened to me when I read the Miller quote above (and the rest of the book). It was the most wonderfully horrible thing to ever happen: brutally painful, disorienting, lonely, confusing, and worth every moment.

Whatever you need to do, it will be worth it. Whatever the price. You already know what it has cost you to live falsely. You pay it every fucking day, all day long, and it kills you a little bit more each day. Actually kills you.

You have never had the words to describe it, to make other people understand. So you shut up and hide even the agony of hiding yourself. But your temper is getting worse, or your depression, or both. You wonder if you need drugs, but you don't want them. You just want to feel...something you can't name.

I will name it for you.

You want to feel what it's like to live as yourself.

Jesus, you can't imagine what that is, but you have the sense it must be better. And you are right.

> Like it or not, you must make a new mental map of where you are. You must become Robinson Crusoe, or you will die. To survive, you must find yourself. Then it won't matter where you are. – Laurence Gonzales, *Deep Surviva*l

People won't like it when you do this. Some of them, anyway. Fuck those people. They want you broken and hobbled, and willing to sacrifice your very life to keep them from the slightest discomfort. Fuck them all.

You are worth being yourself. You deserve it. But only you can decide to have it. Nobody can give it to you. At this stage of life, it must be earned.

Understand the price might include, well, everything and everyone. Not necessarily, but if you aren't willing to pay that price, then you will hedge and hamper your own efforts. Some people will self-select out of your life, while others will show up, drawn by the attraction of your authentic self.

If this book is anything, it is a record of what I have learned on that self-same path. I present it to you in hopes that my experiences might, just maybe, help in some small way.

Good luck to you

Madness

The map is not the territory. – John Grinder

Seventy-five high school seniors ran through the Sonora desert, and a dozen of them were about to get lost.

I trailed twenty yards behind the knot of jocks jogging with ease. They had boasted amongst themselves who would win the 10k race. I was already gasping fifteen minutes into the race. I'd never been a distance runner, and that wasn't about to change.

We were in a surprisingly dense thicket of scrub trees, cacti, and shrubs, on a vague dusty road. I was ahead of the mass of non-jock kids but behind the jocks, who were laughing and shoving each other. They had every right to feel confident in their physical abilities, but suddenly I saw they had made a mistake.

A very serious mistake.

I stopped and stared at the ribbon of cotton tied to a branch a few feet down the even smaller road to the right, and another a bit farther still. The route was marked *that way*, but the guys forged ahead on the same road we started on.

I gave a shout and pointed. One of them turned and waved, but they kept going.

I turned to the kids coming up behind me, pointed at the little flag and took off down the right path, checking behind me to make sure I was followed.

They followed my turn to the right.

I take exception to the tired definition that insanity is doing the same thing over and over expecting different results. People don't bother to examine what those words originally meant. What is wrong with you people? Think about shit now and then, don't just laugh and repeat it.

Here's a much simpler definition I just now made up for the purposes of this chapter.

INSANITY IS THE REFUSAL TO ACCEPT REALITY.

Maybe somebody else thought of it before me. I don't know. Or care.

You can see how the earlier maxim encompasses this definition, right? Please don't make me spoon feed you every fucking detail. I'm not your babysitter. Feed yourself.

The thing is, people die from this kind of insanity every year, all over the world. They get lost. They don't know where they are, physically, but they refuse to accept the reality that is about to kick their asses into the hereafter.

The first part of reality is that Nature is a fucking psycho bitch, and she wants us all dead. Get that into your head, and it might save your life one day.

The weather that day was warm, but not dangerous on its own. We were expected to complete the run by noon. Nobody brought water.

I had been momentarily tempted to try catching up with the race leaders, but quickly realized that was a bad idea. First, there was every chance they wouldn't let me close the gap but would instead pour on the steam as I approached. Second, even if I did catch them, I don't know if I could have convinced them to turn around.

(Backtracking is almost never done in survival situations, even though it could save your life. Runaways won't go back home, abusive victims won't leave, and they end up dying from it.)

And finally, by going after them, I would have caused the bulk of the kids to also go the wrong direction and end up who knows where. We were already miles and miles from the nearest human structure.

Instead, I decided to follow the correct path and report the mistake of the lost boys at the finish. They would probably need to be rescued, and it would happen much faster this way.

The dirt path eventually returned to the gravel road, and half a mile ahead were the buses waiting for us. I finished in first place.

Yay.

It eventually became clear that the athletes weren't going to make it on their own, so one of the buses was dispatched to find them. The sun was thinking about taking a dip in the Sea of Cortez by the time the exhausted, dehydrated, and sunburned lads were picked up trying to find their way back to the main road.

They had just kept fucking running until the road ended. They had not even bothered to wonder about their route until then. Arguments broke out about what to do. Stay put? Go back to the main road? Try to find the turn they missed? What if they didn't find it before the sun went down?

The question we can ask is, "What if the little dirt road had just kept going?"

There was a brief time in recent history when military aircraft used Inertial Guidance Systems (IGS). The concept was that you put the jet on the crosshairs of a location with known geographic coordinates then the plane would keep track of its own movements in relation to that spot and, thereby, be able to calculate its position anywhere in the world.

This was obviated by the deployment of GPS satellites, but for a couple of decades it was the state-of-the-art for navigation. Want to know something really, really cool about mammals?

We have the same thing. We have a neurological IGS.

This is how we know where we are in the world, how we can make our way through our bedroom in the dark (or blind). Cells in the hippocampus (among others) are responsible for this activity. No, the hippocampus is not a school for fat, aquatic quadrupeds. It's a crucial part of the brain, believed to be in charge of emotion, memory, and keeping track of where we are.

When we get lost, reality stops lining up with our mental map of the world. We expect to see a lake over there, but there isn't one, for example. And this is where trouble begins. In his book *Deep Survival*, Laurence Gonzales explains what it feels like to be lost.

> Since the organism's survival depends on a reasonable match between mental map and environment, as the two diverge, the hippocampus spins its wheels and the amygdala sends out alarm signals even as the motivational circuits urge you on and on. The result is vertigo, claustrophobia, panic, and wasted motion. Since most people aren't conscious of the process, there's no way to reflect on what's happening. All you know is that it feels like you're going mad.

We must know where we are in the physical world, but we also need to know where we are symbolically in relation to other people. Where we are in our careers and jobs. Where we are in life. We keep mental maps of all these things, just like we do for the physical world.

Things change all the time in our lives, but sometimes we don't update our mental maps to reflect those changes. The catastrophic loss of a loved one is impossible to process right away. It takes a long time; sometimes it never happens.

Other, less monumental, events happen all the time. The ability to keep our mental maps updated with these changes impacts our very sanity. People fuck this shit up every day. They keep reality and their mental maps from ever meeting. And it makes them crazy.

Like, fucking nuts.

Are you so used to being called crazy that you kind of embrace it? Unless you have a brain injury or fucked-up brain chemistry, it doesn't have to be that way.

The lost boys were so confident, they never allowed reality to interfere with their good times. Only the fortunate accident of reaching the end of the road saved them from even worse circumstances.

We do this shit all the time, the same fucking shit, but not just with wandering off and getting lost. We do it with our relationships, with our jobs, with our families, with damn near every part of our lives.

We miss the flags telling us to take a turn and then we end up in places we don't recognize but we persist in believing we're on the right path, despite overwhelming evidence to the contrary.

Reality isn't for wimps.

The easy thing is to deny the reality around you while scorching everyone to cinders with your blamethrower. Or wish *really, really* hard that the reality everyone else experiences isn't the *real* reality. Or insist this isn't the life you are supposed to be living.

So, you walk around acting as if reality is your bitch, instead of the other way around. But the Universe doesn't give a fuck what you want. It's busy building galaxies and shit. This is the point where people start calling you crazy. Because you *are* fucking crazy. The longer you hold reality at bay, the crazier you get.

And not in a cute way.

In a survival situation (a.k.a. life) the sooner you accept reality, the better the chance of getting through it.

Accepting reality does not preclude acting to alter it. In fact, it's a requirement. I might wish weeds wouldn't grow in my lawn, but that doesn't seem to prevent them from thriving. There are things I can do once I accept the reality of weeds, but not before.

Pretending, wishing, and other fun ways of avoiding the acknowledgment of reality just makes you more and more fucking nuts without the benefit of improving one goddamn thing.

But maybe that's what you're into.

You Don't Know Shit

When I was a lad of twelve, one of my married sisters would invite my parents to her house for Sunday dinners once a month. The forty-minute drive was torture to an ADD kid, especially since my dad drove maddeningly slowly.

The time was spent looking out the window of the car, watching *everyone* pass us. I swear to Odin, I saw a three-legged dog run past us on the freeway. If you are going to ask why I didn't take along a book to read, just shut up. I don't know why, OK? Happy now?

Sometimes I would observe the people in other cars just a couple yards away. They were close enough to notice their clothing, hair, facial expressions. One day an insight struck me: I have no idea what it's like in that other car.

Not the physical environment, though. Not the interior. What the fuck does that matter? I mean, what was the experience of being with those people? It was not possible to know what was happening, what it was like in that other vehicle, without being there.

This is one of those things that is so obvious *we forget we know it*. We take fragments of information about others and extrapolate it into entire universes of assumptions. All the while bitching like a crackhead who lost her pipe when other people make assumptions about us.

You don't know what a situation was like unless you were standing right-fucking-there at the time.

You do not get to decide how someone should react to an event in their life.

You don't have a clue why you do the shit you do, so stop expecting other people to make sense.

You don't know what it's like being anyone but yourself. At best.

In short, when it comes to other people, you really don't know shit. So, cut them a break because you are sure as hell going to ask for one eventually.

It's Complicated

1. Do more of what works.
2. Do less of what doesn't work.
3. Try new things.

These are the principles that guided the founders of Neuro-Linguistic Programming (NLP), Richard Bandler and the other guy. Oh, yeah, John Grinder (thanks, Google!). This is how pragmatism operates in a person's life.
If the thing works, woohoo! Keep doing that shit.
If the thing doesn't work, boo! Knock that shit off.
Hey, here's a new thing. Let's see what happens when I do it. This will provide feedback which will take you to either #1 or #2.

Now, this is harder to do than it sounds because people are messed up, and they like to complicate the shit out of every little thing.
We seem, as a species, deeply dedicated to the idea that if we keep doing something long and hard enough, sooner or later it will bend to the overwhelming might of our persistence and *finally* cough up the results we have wished for.

We think we can be perfect enough so that our spouse will love us and then they will stop abusing us.

We think we can be successful in a field where we really aren't that good, and not much interested in doing what it takes to become that good.

We think we can say the right words and all the badness in the world will vanish.

We think we can order our lives to avoid ever being hurt (or triggered, or embarrassed, or shamed, or…) again.

How has that worked out for you so far?

I have a pretty good idea because you're reading this book. But if you're hoping to find words for your self-delusion and self-justification, then I have one thing to say to you.

Ooopsie!

You don't need me for that. Tons of blogs, websites, and Facebook groups can be found to soothe your sunburned ego and help you understand that your life is not your fault. But I haz news for you.

It doesn't matter whose fault it is – *your life is now your responsibility.*

Whoa, now, wait just a second before you say, "Duh!" because somewhere, in some aspect or respect, you've been pawning off responsibility to others. You might call it by some other name, but it all comes down to pushing the blame outward onto some poor bastard who hurt your feels. Really bad, I'm sure.

Every single time you say shit like, "I can't because—" you are blaming your life on someone else. So? Blame isn't simply ducking personal responsibility, it is surrendering your personal power to the target of your blame.

Tell me, then, if that person is so godawful, why the hell would you want them owning a piece of your power?

Then again, some people derive perverse rewards from doing shit that doesn't work. These are the drama queens, the attention whores, the martyrs. Having their lives be one constant string of China Syndromes (look it up) after another is the only way they know how to get the attention they crave like a junkie.

Escaping the mire of self-delusion requires being brutally honest with yourself in a way you may not have done before.

Oh, I have no doubt you are aces at berating and beating up on yourself. I'm not talking about that. I mean, just be honest without any fucking drama. Without explaining or justifying.

OK, fine, I will provide a personal example. But only because you asked so nicely.

I struggle during conversations to keep on topic. It's a real thing and a real challenge because everything the other person says reminds me of (at least) one other thing that may only be related to the subject in the broadest of definitions.

On top of that, if I don't say it right away, chances are it will be lost down the memory hole forever, so I feel compelled to interrupt with my magical little grain of trivia that is, *at most*, only interesting to me.

Some people find it rude, and they are probably right, even though to me it is a sign of an engaging conversation. When I was dating, I learned to forewarn women about this trait.

It didn't help, but that's a different topic.

Whenever someone says, "It's complicated" about some aspect of their life (and not Quantum Mechanics) it means "I know what the answer is, but I really don't want it to be the answer, so I'm busy pretending there is some other answer I like better."

Often the complication is leaving. Job, family, city, relationships, friends. Those may well be difficult things, but they aren't complicated. They're just hard.

[*Are we getting back to the subject of this chapter anytime soon?* – Editor]

[*Give me your Adderall, bitch* – SK]

Pretending can be a useful tool, but only when you are using it deliberately. Pretending (a.k.a, practicing) is how we develop new skills. Pretending to have a boyfriend is how you end up losing friends and looking crazy. Yes, even in a romantic comedy.

Look, it's reeelly simple. If you want to make progress in your life, you have to be honest with yourself about #1 and #2 or else #3 won't do you any good. At all.

Alrighty, then, let's see what's up next.

Stereotypes Are Important

Tell me if you've heard that stereotypes are bad. Like, always bad. In every case and situation.

Also, that generalizations are the same as stereotypes. Anyone who stoops to the use of a generalization is a bigoted person who is very naughty. [*And not in the good way.* – SK]

Bad, bad, and even more badder.

So, let's pretend you are wandering in the tall grass of the Mara Plains in Kenya when you happen to spot the flick of a lion's tale. No, not in the distance. It's so close, you pee your pants. Or want to, at a bare minimum.

But then you stop yourself. It's unfair to judge lions by their stereotypes. This one might not want to eat you. It could be a vegan lion. Locally sourced and gluten-free, of course. Although you now feel ashamed for being so quick to judge this lion based on nothing more than generalizations, you also still want to pee yourself.

Why the internal conflict? Because generalizations have developed over eons to serve a very useful purpose: so we don't have to learn about the individual inclinations of every fucking lion and leopard. Big cats like to kill and eat things, and it serves our personal survival to keep that well in mind.

"But," you argue, because you always fucking argue, "People aren't the same as animals. You can't generalize about people!"

Oh, yes you can. And you do. Even you.

And there is nothing wrong with using stereotypes to judge *groups* of people. No, don't take my word for it.

In 2016, Lee Jussim wrote about his search for the origins of the "stereotypes are bad" dictum in psychological papers. What he found was, well, read it for yourself. (Truth in Stereotypes, see Resources)

> When I first began my research, I had assumed all those social scientists declaring stereotypes to be inaccurate were right. I wanted to know the basis for those claims – not to refute them, but to promote them and proclaim to the world the hard scientific data showing that stereotypes were wrong. So, when some published article cited some source as evidence that stereotypes were inaccurate, I would track down the source hoping to get the evidence.
>
> And, slowly, over many years, I made a discovery: there wasn't any evidence there. Claims of stereotype inaccuracy were based on… nothing. For example, a classic paper from 1977 describing research by social psychologists Mark Snyder, Elizabeth Tanke, and Ellen Berscheid stated: 'Stereotypes are often inaccurate.' Ok, but scientific articles are usually required to support such claims, typically via a citation to a source providing the evidence. This is important so that anyone can find the evidence for such a claim. There is no source here.

In addition, his examination of the research into stereotypes found that people are pretty damn accurate when applying stereotypes to groups.

Go ahead and read the full article. I dare you.

The problem arises when we assume that a group stereotype always fits every individual in the group. It does not.

Look at you getting all red in the face already! That's so adorable. This book is going to give you a heart attack if you can't open your brain to let in some light and fresh air. Doesn't make any difference to me, but there might be people in your life who care about you. It could happen.

I heard (and believed) the same bullshit about stereotypes, too, same as you. But then my views were changed by actual research. It wasn't important to me that I was right. It was important to know what was right.

Now, if I make a generalization in this book [*More like when.* – Editor] you will know I am talking about a stereotype for a group, with full knowledge and awareness that it does not apply to every member of said group without me having to fucking say this every goddamn time.

You have no chance of remembering this, do you?

Your Worth Runs Your Life

Anyone who has been owned by a lawn knows you can't get rid of dandelions by mowing them down. You can cut the tops off, sure, but those motherfucking roots run deep. Seems obvious, right?

So why the fuck do we spend so much time and effort dealing with our emotional dandelions with a weed whacker? (It's a metaphor, for gawd's sake.)

Yes, people are lazy, stupid, and afraid (present company excepted—or is it especially?) but what else is at play?

Like dandelions in the lawn, the roots aren't visible, yet we live everyday with the myriad ways shitty self-worth expresses itself in our lives.

After many long, deep, probing (no, not that) conversations and introspection, I have come to the conclusion that damn near every problem we have in our lives can be traced back to having shitty (or no) self-worth.

In fact, to make things simple let's just say all your problems are caused by your lack of self-worth because if you fixed those, you would think you had the most amazing life ever in the world and whatever remained would seem trivial.

Things Your Worth Fucks Up

I'm hard pressed to come up with an aspect of relationship fuck-ups that don't trace back to self-worth.

Like constantly choosing partners that cause more harm than good. Like feelings of jealousy, fear of abandonment, all the stupid insecurities about our partners. Like sabotaging a good relationship. Like remaining in an abusive relationship and/or repeatedly finding abusive partners.

Lack of self-worth keeps some people stuck in adolescence as emotional cripples. Often these people become controlling assholes or manipulative bitches.

Addiction often has roots in trauma, especially the kind of trauma that teaches us we have no value except as victims. The drug of choice is the tool to escape from the trauma, while the lack of worth allows us to do harm to ourselves.

Shitty self-worth causes us to fail to see the true nature of others and ourselves. And if you think I only mean the shit heads of the world, you are not paying attention. Being a zero causes us to misunderstand good people, too, and to misinterpret their intentions and actions in the worst possible way.

We scatter booby traps and land mines all over our relationships, even the best ones. Especially the best ones. That's how fucked up we are.

Of course, since we are certain of our righteousness when we fuck up a good relationship, we completely fail to see our part in wrecking things.

Get the idea? All the fucked-up shit you bitch about in your relationships are things you do to *prove* the value that was put on you as a child.

Where the Fuck Does Self-Worth Come From?

This was the question put to my awesome therapist, Doc Awesome [*Not her real name.* – Editor] five years ago. My self-worth was barely measurable. I didn't yet realize just how many things were affected by that, but I knew of several important ones.

I knew it would fuck up any chances of finding a great woman after my divorce, and that was motivation enough for me to want to fix that shit.

This is what I learned about how our worth is instilled in us as we grow up:

As children, we see our worth reflected back to us in the eyes of our parents. – Doc Awesome

Our parents teach us our worth through verbal and nonverbal communications. Especially as infants and toddlers, we see it in their eyes, in their faces. Later, our value is reinforced through thousands of words and actions from our parents.

It would be impossible to enumerate the ways this is done, but every single one of us can name moments when our worth was made abundantly clear, whether it was high, low, or zero.

What the Fuck Do I Do Now?

If you are among the billions of people who grew up thinking your worth was nothing, it might seem like there is little to be done about it other than repeating some weak-assed mantras and affirmations.

Social media is choking on memes that try to help people realize their true value, but nice as they are, they don't do shit beyond provide a moment of good feels.

However, Doc Awesome provided a monumental piece of information about what can be done as adults to correct the misinformation we learned as children:

When we take care of ourselves, especially when we don't feel like it, we prove our own worth to ourselves.

This was such a Holy Shit moment for me that I had to take a moment to write it down, but I am confident that quote will never leave me. Even today, it kinda chokes me up to read it. It was a turning point in my life.

The statement contains several crucial elements.

As nominal adults, we have a way to change our early programming. We aren't helpless victims destined to live with fucked-up self-worth with no way out.

It starts with how we treat ourselves. Not how others treat us, not how we treat others. How we fucking treat ourselves.

We must prove our worth to ourselves. This is the Holy of Holy Shits. More on this in a later chapter, but let this concept sink in for a moment.

This comes with a real bastard of a Catch-22, however.

You need to dig up at least some value in yourself to begin proving your worth to yourself.

The good news is you already are doing it, but your mind isn't giving you proper credit for it. Hang on a little bit longer and I will teach you how to get self-worth.

You Have to Be Wrong to Get Right

People would rather die than be wrong.

Think I'm kidding?

Cockpit voice recorders recovered after airline crashes show time and again that when the captain makes a life-threatening error, the crew will usually sit there without correcting him. They will be silent, even knowing it will kill everybody on board.

They all die because the fucking captain has too big of an ego to admit he has made a mistake. He has berated crew members time and again until they refuse to save their own lives. Surgeons cut off the wrong limbs, or remove the wrong organs, for the same reason.

Right now, you're thinking, "I'm neither a captain nor a surgeon, so what does this chapter have to do with me?"

Because you're just as much of an asshole when you're wrong. That's what.

Those airline captains went down in literal flames believing the entire time they were right. Just like you did today when someone tried to point out a mistake you made.

You wouldn't hear of it. Argued, um, *enthusiastically* for why you were right.

Then you got back to your desk and found out you were wrong the whole time.

How do you react when someone points out one of your limitless number of flaws? You take it in stride with grace and poise, thanking the person for their insights. Right? Bullshit! You handle it with the grace of a figure skater who left all her teeth stuck in the ice.

You defend your precious fucked-up personality as if it were the Hope Diamond. All the knives come out. Nobody gets to call you on your shit. Not even you. Even though industrial grade diamonds have fewer inclusions than you do.

Five minutes later, you pour a drink to numb the pain of your miserable life and can't understand why it isn't better.

Want the simple answer? Well, you're getting it anyway. Shut up and listen.

You will never improve until you can stand to be wrong.

And be wrong a lot.

You watch people on TV, and you see the results of years of hard work. You don't see the work. You don't see where they started out. You don't see the countless mistakes they made along the way.

Picasso wasn't born Picasso, if you get my meaning. He had to learn how. Learning and practicing are designed for mistakes. They are supposed to happen.

Being wrong can kill you. It can make you kill other people. Physically kill people. It can also wreck your relationships with partners, children, and coworkers. It can wreck what little value remains in your sad life, if you persist in your stupid-ass wrongness.

No matter how certain you are of being right, you are probably wrong. I don't give a fuck how sure you are, you are going to be proven wrong sooner or later. In fact, the strength of your certainty is the measure of how fucking wrong you are. Get ahead of the game and let go of that shit now.

Science is a great source of wrongness. That is kind of built into the process. Science doesn't deal in truths, but in theories, with the understanding that it tries to be a little bit less wrong today than it was yesterday.

For just one example, not so long ago, people were murdered to protect the "fact" that the earth was the center of the universe. Certain rulers/administrators felt killing heretics was a small price to pay to preserve the illusion of being right.

But the new way of understanding the stars emerged anyway. And there was much rejoicing.

Except it was still wrong.

The earth is not the center of the universe. But neither is the sun.

Ooops.

Being wrong is important. It's vital to your development that you get to be wrong, that you expect to be wrong.

Here's the deal. You can give up on yourself and accept you will always be the heaping pile of semi-solid fluids you are today. If this is your choice, then shut up about why nothing works out for you.

Or you can start embracing how fucking wrong you are and have been. But also shut up. Nobody wants to hear you whine.

Once you can admit to yourself and others that you've been stupidly, embarrassingly, wrong about every fucking thing, then you can begin to ask the important questions. And then be open to what the answers might be.

What are the important questions? Oh, that's a different chapter.

Why Making Changes Feels Like Dying

Ugh.

I could find some quotes and shit to back this up, but it really isn't necessary. This stuff is obvious once it is explained. And it's simple as fuck.

Yay! Short chapter time!

One of our strongest drives, outside of sex, is to be understood.

We crave it in our bones. We do all kinds of goofy shit to belong to a tribe that understands us. We want, more than anything, to have a partner who gets us.

We are desperate to be understood.

Back in the good old tribal days, everyone understood each other in the tribe. The traditions and the clothes, the food and the living quarters—all these things helped provide a shorthand for identifying people who belonged.

Belonging to the tribe meant safety. It meant life itself, through protection and provisions.

Making a significant personal change that put a person at odds with what the tribe understood put everything at risk.

Stepping too far outside of what the tribe understood meant rejection.

Rejection from the tribe meant living alone.

Living alone meant death.

Actual physical death.

Today, if we get rejected from a club or group, we won't die. But we still feel that potential outcome in our guts.

An ancient part of our brains warns us that making changes will mean people in our tribe won't understand us, and they will kick us out into the fucking wilds, and we will die. This lesson has been etched into our minds since humans banded together.

It has always been the case that when we start to make significant improvements, our tribe will do everything they can to keep us in line with traditions, so we can stay in the tribe.

And still today, when we change enough, we must leave one tribe and seek out another. But it is almost never a life-threatening situation.

It's not easy to overcome this instinct-level programming. But it can be done by making changes and not dying. Do that enough times and you start to believe it.

Dying to Be Seen

In the opening to the book *Ikigai*, author Sebastian Marshall recounts a time when he got off a train at the wrong station in suburban Japan. If this was you or me, there would be no story to tell. We'd get off in a panic and try to find the right train, so we could get where we wanted to go.

But not Mr. Marshall. Oh, no.

He sits down to contemplate. He wants to know the reason he is there, the reason he got on the wrong train and the reason why he got off at this specific station. Those are outstanding questions.

Several trains he should take came and went, yet he remained. Afternoon walked towards evening, and still he sat, consumed by thought.

And then, finally, the epiphany.

> But I arrived here and I hear the birds and cicadas, and I see all the wonderful green land and clean air, and I see these wonderful, nice, kind people living their lives, and who all really harmoniously truly understand each other.
>
> And I got it.
>
> It clicked.
>
> I don't get to have this.
>
> I don't get to have this.

> I get something else. Something pretty amazing. But I don't get to have normal life.
>
> And it looks really, really nice. A lot less neurosis and conflict and striving and fighting forwards.
>
> [....]
>
> But the more you do, the further away you get from being understood, from the joys of normal life, from being understood by your neighbors and backing each other up and living together harmoniously.
>
> I cried for the first time in three years when I realized it.
>
> The million dollar question ... why don't people take the large opportunities in front of them? Why don't they allow their dreams to become realities? Because it means you won't be understood. And we need to be understood, fundamentally, it's so important to us.

Being understood is one of the strongest drives we possess as humans, and yet it gets little acknowledgment.

What, after all, is this idea of compatibility we seek in relationships, if not a sense of mutual understanding? We go to great lengths to be with people who understand us. Where we live, what kind of work we do, who we hang out with and where, how we dress, how we speak.

We need to belong, but only when we belong to a group that understands us.

When we make personal changes, we are no longer understood by our current tribe, so we either seek a new tribe or we revert to our old ways.

Stop Asking Stupid Questions

Contrary to what your nose-wiping babysitters in public high school taught you, there really are such things as stupid questions. There are a lot of fucking stupid questions. But that's ok.

There must be stupid questions. Meaning, it is a requirement, otherwise we can't have really great questions. Great questions are vital to a growing individual.

The reason great questions are so important is because you can't get great fucking answers from stupid questions.

Let's be clear. There is sometimes a distinction between a stupid question and one that appears obvious. Sometimes people make assumptions about the obvious things and forget to ask questions about them. In those cases, asking a question that seems fucking obvious might be a question nobody bothered to ask.

So that would make it a great question.

Lots of times, we make a statement but frame it like a question. These are called presuppositions. It means that we have pre-supposed the answer already. We have decided the answer ahead of time, but we want to appear to be open to other answers.

You can turn a stupid presupposition into a great question while keeping the same words.

Imagine that Newton-guy napping in the orchard when an apple bonks him on the head. If Newton were a typical idiot, he might have exclaimed, "Why the fuck did that apple bonk me on the fuckin' noggin?"

Then he'd rub his head and go back to sleep because the presupposition was that nobody knew why. Apples just fell. That's what they do.

But Newton was more than an icky fruit-filled cookie. Oh yes. He was a rather bright fellow, it turns out.

So, when Newton shouted, "Why the fuck did that apple bonk me on the fuckin' noggin?" he wanted the real answer to the real question he had. [*Citation needed* – Editor] [*I got your citation right here* – SK]

Why did the apple fall down? Why didn't it fall up? Why did it have to fall at all?

Them thar be some mighty fine questions that led to some even mightier and fine-ier answers. See the difference it can make to turn a presupposition into a question? It can get you into the movies! Eventually. Long after you're dead and don't care.

But still.

Who knows? There might be some other piddling benefits, too. (See what I did there?)

If you are wondering what the point is of asking a really great question when you have more problems than a 400-level math book, then you've come to the right place. Lemme make it simple enough for even you to understand.

I mean you there, on the left, not you in the middle. You're hopeless. But for you on the left, pay attention. Are your attention fees fully paid up? Come on, you're making the whole class wait.

Ready? I mean, really, sooper-dooper ready, down to yer bonez ready? Here goes.

You can't get different answers until you ask different questions.

Whoever said "duh" is to report to the underworld demons for a mid-level torture session and chair massage. Of doom.

That statement above certainly sounds obvious, but did you know it? Of course not. Which is weird because there's a chance you have actually done that. But not often enough for it to make an impression on your granite skull.

Take a look.

"Why do women reject me? What the fuck do they really want?"

This is a bit of self-pity at first glance. Certainly not the kind of thinking I would ever engage in. [*We have documentation.* – Editor]

While the current wording of that question [*Bite me.* – SK] could lead one to some valuable insights, with a little bit of adjustment, a whole new universe opens up.

"What do women need in a partner, deep down in their genes?"

This is the kind of question that can lead a person to go out and find answers. And you goddamn better get off your ass and find them after going through the trouble of identifying an important question.

There have been many times flipping a question around has led to entirely new ways of looking at a problem.

Many years ago, the company I worked for faced a serious performance issue with their primary software product. It was bad. As in *bad*. As in, customers were about to cancel huge contracts bad.

I was new on the job; I didn't have much assigned to me, so I decided to look at the performance issue. Identifying the problem was easy, but what to do about it was much more open.

The second day, as I sat on my porcelain meditation throne, I asked an important question: what should the fastest operation be in this process?

Once I had that answer, I wondered what would happen if I took the way the processing was done and completely flipped it around. And if I did that, what would it look like? How would it work?

I drew a few diagrams on the whiteboard to get the concept down. Then I wrote some simple code as a proof of concept. The speed was almost unmeasurable. And it kept being lightning fast even as the complexity grew.

Without realizing it, I had reinvented the trie structure, a match algorithm taught in Masters-level Computer Science courses. My diagrams looked the same, too, except oriented differently. The solution was shockingly fast and allowed the addition of many additional features to the product.

Whatever problem we face, we keep ourselves chained to it when we limit our thinking with dumbass presuppositions and rehashing the same old questions.

Don't ask why she left you, or why bad things keep happening to you, or why you keep attracting the same kinds of losers, unless you want the fucking answer. If you like being stuck, then just shut the fuck up and stop pretending to want to live a better life.

But if you do want something better than your fucking miserable life, change the questions you ask yourself.

Then go find the fucking answers.

Oh, My Fucking Guilt

In the years leading up to kindergarten, my mother used nap time to work on her brainwashing techniques.

Ha ha ha, ur funny, SK.

I mean actual brainwashing. And stop using ur like an illiterate opossum. [*Are there literate opossums?* – Editor] [*Shut it. All the way.* – SK]

"Promise mommy you will always be my boy and not grow up to be like other boys who become ungrateful and leave their mommies," she would plead.

Being a small child, of course I promised. Over and over and over again.

Of course, I didn't keep the promises made as a five-year-old. She expected me to, however, and one time tried to guilt me into it. Either she wasn't very good at brainwashing, or I developed enough sense of self, barely, to resist.

[Lots of arguing and yelling]

"You promised to never become like this!" she scolded.

"I was a baby!"

This pissed her off even more. All her efforts down the shitter because I wouldn't play the game.

The game called Guilt.

It's a simple game with very few rules.

A variety of authority figures instill a sense of shame, then spread that to whatever behaviors they want to manipulate in you. They are often boiled down to simple words that are jammed full of guilt.

Skank. Slut. Whore. Bitch. The list can go on and on. It isn't just sexual behavior, but that is common with a host of guilt-words.

Make no mistake about it, guilt is fucking emotional blackmail. It is emotional manipulation designed to force you to behave the way others want you to. It is immoral and unjustifiable.

The fuckers realize their demands are stupid as shit, and that any rational person would laugh in their faces. But they want you to behave differently to suit their own purposes, so they pull out the guilt card.

They rely on it to work without question. Not questioning is the foundation of guilt. The last thing they want you to know is what I'm about to tell you.

You don't have to play.

It is voluntary. You play by choice. No matter how deep the hooks were set you can liberate yourself by simply refusing to play.

They will even try to guilt you into staying in the guilt game. How meta is that?

The emotions you feel when participating in guilt aren't real. They aren't your own. They were pushed onto to you for later manipulation.

Freeing yourself from the game is a two-step process. You've already done the first part by learning the true nature of guilt. Becoming aware of how guilt works in your life, and who is pulling which strings, is like waking up from a three-day bender in Nogales. You don't know how the fuck you got there, or what you did, but now it's time to find a way home.

And some antibiotics are probably a good idea.

Here is the only other step you need to do to get out of the game.

Own your shit.

Take full responsibility for your choices and their consequences. The guilt-trippers depend on you feeling shame. It's all they have.

When you own your shit and they call you a slut, just think to yourself, "So?"

Even better, say it.

In fact, "So?" is the magic bomb disposal technique for all guilt attempts. They have no response to it. None. It breaks from the script. It breaks their brains. They can't even.

Holy fuck it is fun to say and watch the reactions.

Quit the game. Experience the freedom of keeping guilt out of your life.

Do it today.

Quitting Time

December of my senior year of high school, I'm sitting in Mr. Ziegler's fourth period psychology class, listening to a very inspired speech about his special "seminar" for seniors. This had been going on all semester, but today he was really into it.

I don't remember his words, only that suddenly I felt the urge to sign up. Joining seminar was the easy part, though.

I would have to quit *Fiddler on the Roof* two weeks into rehearsals. I would have to quit a play. That just wasn't done in my world. I mean, not done *ever*.

Quitting has very negative connotations. Breaking up is quitting. Divorce is quitting. Leaving a job is quitting. Sometimes we need to quit, but the Roolz about when it's okay to quit and when it is not okay are murky and conflicting.

That day in high school, I didn't know what to do. I'd been in the performing arts for fifteen years already. People who quit plays were not good, not reliable people. Yet, I felt an urgent need to participate in the seminar. It was truly a once in a lifetime opportunity and something quite outside of what had been my life so far.

I needed to break the mold, break from family tradition. I needed to be my own person. Desperately. And I needed to be a quitter to get what I needed.

The next morning, I asked my oldest brother about quitting. He was busy reading a college textbook and eating.

Without looking up he said, "Never quit just because something is hard. Quit if it isn't taking you where you want to go, not because it's hard." He went back to studying and eating, and I went to school with my answer.

That explanation has served me well ever since because sometimes we need to give ourselves permission to quit and know that it is the right thing.

Peace on Earth

I'm going to tell you something you don't want to hear. [*Now there's a change of pace.* – Editor]

There will never be peace on earth. It is impossible.

We will always have psychopaths/sociopaths. We will always have psychotics.

You can't change them with candles or drums or prayers or good thoughts. You can't change them with laws. You can't talk them out of their conditions. They do not care about other people.

You cannot understand them. Be very clear about this. You do not have the capacity to comprehend their thought mechanisms and be glad of that. Any attempt to fit their actions into the framework of a normal mind is futile.

They do not view themselves as abnormal in any way. On the contrary, they view normal people as being handicapped by emotional constraints.

When bad people decide to do bad things, no law in the world will dissuade them. Laws are only for the law-abiding. Criminals, and those who plan to become criminals don't care about laws. Kinda what makes them criminals.

And when bad people decide to murder, which has been against the law for a while now, the tools they choose are less important to them than the outcome. Take one away, and they will use another, all the way down to rocks and sticks and bare hands.

Why did Nature decide psychopaths were a necessary part of evolution? I can come up with two possibilities. I don't know if there is research to support either of these. I'm simply going on what makes a little bit of sense.

One is that developing emotional connections with other human beings is a recent evolutionary change in the human population which hasn't yet become universal. In this case, psychopathy might eventually breed itself out of the population. I have a lot of doubt about this one because bonding is what made the early tribes survive.

The second option is that psychopathy was added by Nature on purpose. But why?

With every predator on earth, their population is controlled by the amount of available food. This is true of humans as well except we have figured out how to produce food beyond subsistence levels. We are not constrained by the number of Woolly Mammoths in the neighborhood because we can grow wheat and rice and corn and raise cattle.

So maybe, just maybe, Nature gazed upon these clever chimps and decided there needed to be an apex predator above humans. One problem: apex predators take a long time to evolve. And the humans learned how to protect themselves against tigers, and to stay out of the shark's house.

Oh, heh, here's a quick solution: let's make some humans into predators of other humans! Simple and easy. Just leave out the part of the brain that allows them to feel any bond with other humans.

Most psychopaths aren't criminals of any kind and some are even useful to our society. Some become presidents of companies. Some become politicians. Some become firefighters or soldiers or cops. Or salespeople.

But a few develop as predators of humans.

The scale of their hunting grounds depends on countless factors, but the range is staggering, from a one-time murder, to Stalin and Mao. Death by all wars in history are estimated to be up to a billion people.

One billion. That's a thousand million. That's double the number of people in North America.

Fucking psychopaths are the most effective predators Nature has ever created.

And some people just can't wait to be killed by them. I'm talking about pacifists.

Drum circle jerks can't deal with the reality of the world, so they wish really, really hard that people will be different than what they are. They want peace so badly they are willing to sacrifice your very life to their cause.

It's easier for me to understand how psychopaths evolved than the people who prostrate themselves before the psychopaths and hope for mercy. The Omega males and females who show their bellies to the psychopaths. The fucking universe won't protect them from blood-lust because the universe *made* those fuckers precisely to kill other humans.

How you like your loving universe now, bitches?

Cowards have always been among us, and they hold an equivalent culpability to the psychopaths for mass deaths throughout history. Why? Because they fight against their own Warrior Class when their society is threatened by an outside psychopath. They cause delays, try to make deals, try to avoid war, sell out their own people, try to make the wars unwinnable in the name of peace.

But war always comes, and the price of cowardice is always paid with the blood of the warriors and the innocent. War always comes because we always have psychopaths.

The question then is if we can overcome the cowards in society enough to defeat the war mongering psychopaths sooner instead of later.

The Magic Eight Ball® of history says no.

Beauty Is a Beast of a Burden

If only our eyes saw souls instead of bodies how very different our ideals of beauty would be. – Stupid Ass Facebook Meme

Imagine you're at a party and across the room you see The Most Beautiful Woman in The World (TMBWITW). Imagine further that she sees you, too. Your eyes meet and you both cross to each other, then you move off to a quiet corner to chat. You pretend to listen to her, but your heart is about to explode.

Then she tells you she has this idea for super secure wireless communications. What do you do with this information?

Do you believe her?

Women get so fucking weird about the concept of beauty. Come on, you know what I mean. They hate it on other women; or wish they had more of it; or have it but don't realize it; or regret the loss of it when they get older; or hate being noticed for it; or hate not being noticed for it; or get annoyed that men hold onto it longer. Plus, a million variations on the themes.

And all the while, people don't even understand what the purpose of beauty is. They are too busy getting pissy about where they currently fall on the spectrum, compared to where they wish they were, to spare a single neuron to consider the origins of the concept.

Let's take a moment right the fuck now.

Put aside your visceral reactions to the word to contemplate why we have the word 'beauty', and why we apply it to people. Go ahead. I'll be sitting here looking at beautiful women while you think. [*Everyone needs a hobby, I suppose.* – Editor]

For fuck's sake, don't give up already.

Here's the only clue you need: survival of the species.

That's right, geniuses. It's about fucking. But I hear your question. "Men will stick it into any hole. They aren't at all picky. Where does beauty fit into that, smartass?" [*That's Mr. Smartass to you.* – SK]

Are you ready for the answer? Here it comes.

The concept of beauty evolved as shorthand for the collection of *physical* traits that best represent a fertile and healthy woman, one capable of bearing and raising the best possible offspring.

It's really that simple.

Physical symmetry. Shiny hair. Nice hips and full tits. Good teeth. Clear skin. So on, and so on, and scooby-dooby-dooby.

A man wants to perform genetic recombination experiments with the highest quality female available to him. And before you get your bowstring in a knot, women do the same shit with men, but using their own criteria.

Humans have been doing this since always. And women have been giving each other shit about it since always minus one day.

Now talk to me about how enlightened we are today. Go ahead. Tell me.

Frequency-hopping forms the basis of the Wi-Fi technology I'm using to write this. Among many other applications. It was decades ahead of its time. And it was invented by one of the greatest Hollywood beauties of all time, Hedy Lamar. Go ahead, look it up.

She had a tough time being taken seriously because men just wanted to fuck her and not listen to her ideas. They were too stupid to know they could do more of the former, if they also did the latter. Fucking morons.

Here's the problem with beauty when it comes to finding a partner: competition. Beauty establishes a value structure for females, and the competition among males is for the highest value female they can attract.

[*Look, I didn't invent the concept of "high value females", so just because it pisses you off doesn't make it invalid.* – SK]

Men tend to aim high. Like way too high. The term "out of his league" was invented for such men.

At the same time, some women love being fought over. On occasion, they want actual combat. There is a technical term for these women: *fucking nuts*. Avoid at all costs.

I did the online dating thing for a couple of years. It's really fucked up, the whole process. One thing it highlights is the competition over high value females because every man on the site carpet bombs women with emails. Usually the same email sent to every good-looking woman on the site.

I heard first hand stories of women who were buried under mountains of emails. Hundreds a day, every day. Pretty revolting stuff, too.

Men get frustrated when, time after time, the women they pursue fail to respond in a like manner. It can be deeply frustrating and discouraging. And also unnecessary.

Pay attention, you chumstick creepers and dick-lint InCels (involuntary celibates).

Women owe you *nothing* just because you exist. Get over yourselves. If you aren't getting laid, that's your problem and not theirs. The more you try to make it their problem the worse things will get for you. It turns into a self-fulfilling prophecy.

One mistake you make is to throw your little hook into the same waters as the big boys. The guys you hate because they get all the chicks. I understand those women are very attractive. That's why the competition is so fierce.

Relax, guys. There isn't an actual pussy drought in the world, even if it seems like it. Numerically speaking, there are more women in the USA than men. The problem is one of competition. You know you can't compete with the big boys, so why the fuck are you so stupid? Why do you keep trying for the same women they go after?

Jesus, you guys are fucking idiots.

Want the short version? Not sure I can dumb this down far enough, but I promise to try.

- There is no formula, recipe, code word, or trick that works with women.
- Because women are non-deterministic. Look it up yourself, you lazy bastard.
- When you make women the purpose of your life, you scare the shit out of them. The good ones, at least.
- Lying and other tricks will be found out. And then you will lose her. Did you read any ambiguity in those words? No, because there ain't any.
- Live an interesting life.

- Women dig it when you treat them like real people and not just fuck stations. Did you know they can seem like real people?
- When you allow women to come to you suddenly there isn't any competition. Yes, this works with online dating.
- If your love life isn't going the way you want, fuck it. Take a long break. Focus on being a better person and living your life.
- Play it cool. Be patient. Fucking listen.
- Authenticity is the strongest aphrodisiac on the planet. And it works.

Those are the basics, but here are a few more quick tips: Stop being a fucking whining emo bitch. Stop being a creeper. Stop blaming women.

I'm not saying women are perfect. At all. I'm saying own your shit because you are the only thing you have any control over.

I'm also saying that if you follow my advice, you will find yourself attracting higher quality women than ever before because women get tired, bored, and disgusted by the sheer volume of men trying to fuck them. Especially the beautiful ones.

You think women have an easy life? Ask around, dumbshit. Everyone deals with fucked-up shit, not just you. You are not special, even with your boxes of participation trophies.

At first, I chased the same women online as did all the other guys. Guess how many responded to my messages?

Zero. Exactly.

After a while, I wrote the Best Profile in The World [*Is there some kind of award for this?* – Editor] and then waited to see what would happen. [*If there was, I'd win it.* – SK] It was like going out in a boat and having the fish jump in.

Here's the thing to keep in mind. Women are actual people. They enjoy being valued for things other than their bodies. Not instead of. Also. They like to be appreciated. They like to be loved. They like to be listened to. They have feelings. Just like you.

When a woman does you the fucking favor of showing interest, be a goddamn gentleman about it. Don't be mean to her if you're not interested. Be thankful, you little shit. Word gets around.

Now, there is a great deal more to dating than a clever profile. If you don't know that, just stop now. You are too hopeless to breathe.

Part II: You Suck

The Gory Days

What's the difference between an adult woman and a 14-year-old girl?

The number of years of experience being 14.

I have told that joke to lots of women, and you know what the universal reaction is? "Ha! That is so true! I know women like that!"

Uh huh. It's always someone else.

There is a general distaste among women for other women who behave like they are still in junior high (or middle school, or whatever the hell you call it in your country). Perhaps it's the myopia of introspection that prevents people from seeing themselves as they are. More importantly, why the fuck do so many women get emotionally stuck at that age?

We all know people who keep the same hair style from high school. It's kinda weird, but OK, it doesn't really hurt anyone.

The middle years (especially) of puberty are universally seen as worse than being slowly ground up by a dull paper shredder. That's lubricated with Jalapenos. And infected with rabies. So why the hell would you want to keep reliving one of the worst periods of your life?

For some, they feel a sense of power. Mean-grrrrl power. It was the age when those skills were honed and tempered, if you aspired to them. Manipulation, condescension, and deception are tools of the trade while outwardly complaining loudly about people who play games.

Whatever success was achieved climbing the bitch hierarchy fed the egos and cemented this as their emotional benchmark. These women always have "trust issues" because they are fundamentally untrustworthy. They demand complete honesty while offering their own limited-edition interpretation of it.

For others, the emotional whiplash of puberty provided a rush of adrenaline, especially if their excesses went unchallenged. The more shit the girls got away with, the bigger the rush. The need to learn moderating behaviors only arose from negative consequences. If she never faced any of the latter, then she never learned the former.

These women push boundaries all the time. They spin drama out of thin air but, whereas mean grrrrls make drama to serve a larger goal, the adrenaline junkies are in it for sheer entertainment value.

There is a third group of women.

By some magic formula of environment, nature, and temperament, they come through puberty and emerge on the other side as the rarest of creatures.

Adults.

No, really. They do exist!

If you haven't met one, it doesn't surprise me at all. Richard Attenborough refused to do a documentary on them, saying they were mythical. That's how rare they are.

It has been, and remains, my great fortune to have personal relationships with several such women. (Not counting the ones I helped make.) Let me tell you, brother, life around emotionally adult women is a different universe from the other types.

Men are drawn to them. Other women pretend to be like them for as long as they can pull it off. It's a life where you have the space to think about things besides, "What the fuck will happen today?"

Some of you doubt my veracity. Some of you don't know what veracity means. If I didn't have first-hand experience, I wouldn't believe me, either. Hell, sometimes I wonder if I'm hallucinating the whole thing. [*You aren't the only one.* – Editor]

On the off chance I'm not hallucinating, being around actual adult women is one of the most incredible experiences life has to offer. To quote Ferris Bueller, "It is so choice. If you have the means, I highly recommend picking one up."

Are You A Creeper?

You fucking guys make me crazy.

You read all the women's gripes about creepers, and yet you think, "But I'm not one of those!"

Sorry, pal, but you probably are a fucking creeper.

How do I know? Take this simple test.

- These words are interchangeable to you: male, guy, man
- You have been blocked by at least one woman on social media without explanation
- You can't get a second date
- You have a tough time getting a first date
- You send personal messages to women on social media that you don't know
- You are in a relationship, but try to hook up online with other women
- You tell strange women you love them
- You propose marriage to women you don't know
- You send dick pix without permission
- You get shuffled off to the Friend Zone every fucking time
- You can't understand women

- Everyone of your social and relationship problems were caused by women
- You use the words bitch, twat, and cunt regularly
- When women don't respond the way you want, it makes you angry

If you answered yes to > 1 (that's more than one to you fucking morons) then you are a creeper. Take your medicine, pal, and man up.

Don't worry, though. If you have the balls, I will lead you out of Creeperville and into the land of milk and boobies.

But you don't have the balls, you pussy. Do you? No. You have no spine, you're a wimp and a fucking blamer. You don't own your shit. You want women to bend to your will instead of taking the time to learn about them.

Here's your first lesson.

Women are people. But not like men.

Fucking loser, you think you know that? No, you don't. If you did, you wouldn't be a goddamn creeper. Jesus, lepers have more social capital than you.

Men will learn a thing or two. Guys will be a bit uncomfortable, but a few will learn and grow, and eventually become men. Creepers are the invertebrates of the species. I doubt any will ever develop into guys, much less men.

Prove me wrong. I fucking dare you.

Are You A Bitch?

I really don't care for the word 'bitch' except when referring to female dogs. But I gotta say, some women make it a real challenge to keep that word in the holster. Plus, the word is deeply and cruelly unfair to female dogs, who are almost universally loving and sweet.

Let me tell you what a (human) bitch is, and what it ain't.

A strong woman isn't a bitch because she has no need to put on a show of strength. A strong woman goes about her life without apologies, and without making scenes.

A loving woman isn't a bitch because she knows how to interact with her partner. She doesn't need threats or verbal abuse to make her point.

A kind woman isn't a bitch because, well, those are pretty much opposites.

A smart woman isn't a bitch. She always knows better, and she mostly behaves like she knows better. On those occasions when things get away from her, she fucking *apologizes*.

A determined woman isn't a bitch. She's just determined. Sometimes that determination becomes unreasonable, but men do that shit, too. You don't have to like determined women, but that doesn't mean they are bitches.

A woman who uses sex as a weapon is a bitch. If you even *hint* about this shit, you're a fucking bitch. You don't deserve a good man. I am dead serious.

A woman who thinks she can get away with treating men like shit is a bitch. Sorry, but your snatch isn't some magic cavern filled with fairy sprinkles. It's (at best) the same as every other adult human female. Nothing special about it. Just because you can shake your tits and get guys lining up doesn't make your pussy magical. They all get tired of your shit before long. Or haven't you noticed?

A woman who treats other women like shit is a bitch. I don't care what you think she did.

A woman who stirs up drama just to get her rocks off is a bitch. Drama belongs on the stage. Nobody likes that shit but you.

A woman who thinks the only way to gain power is to take it from other women is a bitch. American Kennel Club certified bitch. See those other women? Nothing about them takes anything away from you. Focus on being you, on fixing your own bullshit. Forget about everyone else.

A woman who yells is a bitch. I mean, come on. Everybody is tired of that shit. Every single body you know hates it. Hates. It. Shut up already.

A woman who resorts to manipulation to get what she wants is a bitch. Like, say, insisting that you always win arguments no matter what. Or waving your tits in the faces of guys to get them to do what you want.

A woman who must always be right is a bitch. Not much else to add to this one.

My suspicion is that many of these bitchy behaviors are fear-based. Perhaps such women fear they really are good for nothing but sex, that they have nothing else to offer in a relationship. Whether or not that is true comes down to individual cases. But it doesn't have to be true for anyone.

Nobody likes bitches. If you have such tendencies, knock it the fuck off. Jesus, the *whole world* is tired to death of this shit.

Nice Guys Suck

A moment ago, I read about a young woman who is struggling to break her pattern of dating guys who are, well, shitheads. She wants to date nice guys, but they scare her because she doesn't trust their motivations. This is what I wrote to her.

I think you are looking for a good man, not a nice guy. They may exhibit similar behaviors at times, but the differences between them are on the inside and they are fundamental to who they are as people.

A good man isn't needy. He wants to be with you, but he doesn't crumble when you're apart. A nice guy depends on you to feel good about himself.

A good man is complete and whole as he is but knows, with the right partner, his life can be richer and fuller. A nice guy needs a partner to feel happy.

A good man leads his own life and is looking for a partner who does the same. A nice guy makes you the center of his life, or he needs to be the center of yours. Or both.

A good man is comfortable being alone. A nice guy becomes anxious when he is forced to spend time by himself.

A good man sees you for who you are. He is curious to know everything about you. A nice guy sees you for what he needs from you.

A good man wants you to see him for who he truly is, flaws and all. A nice guy works overtime to hide his flaws and gets defensive when you notice them.

A good man accepts you as you are right now. Maybe you work out long-term, maybe not, but he has no intention of changing you. A nice guy wants you to fit his vision of an ideal partner.

A good man says what he means, means what he says, but doesn't say it in a mean way. A nice guy will say anything to keep the peace or get what he wants.

A good man will tease you in a playful way. A nice guy will tease to hurt or manipulate you.

When a good man pays you a compliment, it is offered as a gift without strings or expectations. When a nice guy offers a compliment, you wonder what he's after.

A good man behaves as a gentleman because of who he is and what he values. A nice guy tries to be a gentleman because it scores points with you.

A good man tries to improve himself and he takes responsibility for this. A nice guy is looking to be rescued.

A good man enjoys being a man. He is never embarrassed or apologetic about being a man. A nice guy is never sure what being a man means or how to go about it.

What I Hate About Women

I love women and always have. I am 100% pure hetero male. I harbor not a dram of confusion or doubt on this point. Having played sports as a yoot, I saw plenty of nekkid male bodies, and not once did the sight increase blood flow to the old bat & balls. The smile of a beautiful woman, however....

My first girlfriend was Mary. We planned on getting married because that's what young people do. Unfortunately, Mary's family moved away, and I never saw her again.

We were five years old.

Unsurprisingly, the phase where boys are disgusted by girls (roughly ages 0-14) skipped right on by like it owed me money. The most that can be said is that my desire for girls went into hibernation from first through fourth grades.

I was assigned to a split class in fourth grade. Half the class was made of fifth graders. The teacher, Mr. B, provided a strong male role model of the kind that could never teach in the pussyfied K-12 programs of today.

When Mr. B asked for volunteers to work as crossing guards, I raised my hand. I mean, there was one other boy with his hand up but a dozen girls. The math was in my favor.

We wore orange vests, carried wire rods with orange flags on the end that read "STOP" and we served & protected at the only crosswalk within a quarter mile of the school. The weather was often miserable, like a half-hearted but cold monsoon.

Our shifts were time-delimited. So, we stood at our posts for (seemingly) long stretches with nothing to do. This is where I got my first extra-familial lesson about girls.

They have to talk.

Not want to. *Need* to.

And what they need to talk about is relationships. Even at ten years old. Meanwhile, I'm still making parachutes for G.I. Joe from bread bags.

During my first tour of the front, June asked, out of the blue, "Who do you like?"

Leading the witness, yer honor!

It is quite possible that simple question awakened the slumbering giant in me. Oh please, I don't mean that. It ain't no giant. (I mean, it's OK, it's perfectly fine, lovely even according to reports, garnering neither gasps nor laughs.)

I mean, the dormant interest in girls awakened because I had to provide an answer. Obtuse and naive as I was, I could tell that saying "nobody" would only make things worse. So needing to provide a name of who I liked, made me think about who I liked.

Every day we had to talk about crushes. Endlessly. Funny, thinking back, how evasive the girls became when the question was turned against them, he said, brimming with irony.

There was another consequence of working as a crossing guard. MILFs.

There was no such terminology at the time, but for some reason I started to become aware of the women driving past our post. Some of them were gorgeous, which led to checking out all the drivers.

Girl watching remains a pastime to this day. Except not actual girls, but 'adult human female watching' doesn't have the same ring to it.

Anyway, those are a few of my *bona fides* from my childhood. I love women. But it could have turned out differently.

I have a very long list of reasons why I should feel bitter, angry, and other descriptive adjectives, towards women, but it never happened. Through it all, my love and appreciation for women held fast.

It became clear to my young mind that girls were different from boys, and I don't mean tits. Or, not just tits. They acted differently; they spoke differently and about different things; they responded differently and, it seemed, unpredictably.

It was also clear that girls were the ones who decided who they dated. Boys could ask, but they couldn't give orders.

In fact, they would probably have melted if a boy walked up with enough confidence to say, "You're going to Homecoming with me on Saturday. Pick you up at 6."

But none of the boys knew that.

In my world, a boy asked a girl to go out, and she would say yes or no. Or some crueler version of no. Shit, where was I going with this?

Oh, right. I became curious about what made girls tick. What mattered to them, what they thought about, what they wanted.

Thus, began a lifetime of scholarship into the minds of women. It began by simply paying attention and trying to connect more dots than shooting a 12-gauge at a paper target.

It wasn't a constant stream of learning. More like long stretches of nothing punctuated by the occasional insight. But the insights began to pile up.

As my understanding increased, so did my disappointment. Women have so much going for them, but they focus on the wrong fucking things. And they too often prefer to be victims over being responsible for their own situations.

Maybe those apply to men as well but, as I've said many times, I don't date men. And this chapter is about women. So, put away your "yeah, but" darts and just fucking listen for once without making excuses.

I love women enough to insist on seeing them as they are, not as they wish to portray themselves. It's not always positive, but reality is less jolting than fantasy because the latter will eventually shatter.

Here's what I hate about women.

Although I will use the word 'hate' in this context it doesn't mean "intense or passionate dislike." More like things I find a bit annoying. But hate only has four letters, so I have decided to be lazy and use that word. Also, because it will piss off a bunch of readers. It's a twofer!

I hate that women have little sense of their selves as distinct individuals. Their sense of self is nearly always tied up in others. It never occurs to them that it is possible to be a great mom and still be your own self.

One (of many) consequences of the above is that women without a strong sense of self tend to blame others for their situations. This makes sense, in a twisted way. If you aren't a complete individual, then how can you be responsible for what happens to you?

One defense mechanism for the above is this imagined club called The Sisterhood. If it is a club, it's the least exclusive one in the world. The Sisterhood is a source of comfort and anger for women. It's like the blind men trying to guess what animal they have before them (it's an elephant) and each one gives a different answer depending on what part they are touching. Women think The Sisterhood means the same to all other women, and they have a hard time dealing with the rude fact that it doesn't.

I find it annoying that women expect men to understand every aspect of them but make zero effort to understand men. They honestly believe they know everything about men. If that were true, why are there so many unhappy women?

I hate that women claim to want honesty but don't deal with that currency in an equitable manner. Their standards and definition of honesty are too often self-serving, and not at all the same as what they demand of men.

I hate that women treat men, to quote author Alison Armstrong, like "big, hairy, misbehaving women." And I hate how angry they get about it, especially when we don't live up to that unstated demand.

I hate how often women think the only way for them to obtain strength and power is to take it away from others.

I hate how often women believe men have hidden agendas behind our words. We really don't, generally, and the extent to which we do is because we've been burned by women saying they want openness and honesty, only to punish us for doing just that.

I hate when women test men. Think about the times that has worked out well for you. Zero times, right? Why keep doing it? It's fucking stupid, and it's hurting everyone.

I hate that women feel compelled to present as perfect. There's no such thing. And as Anne Lamott said, "Perfection is shallow, unreal, and fatally uninteresting." This is another chapter.

I hate that women are so fixed in their ideas of what an ideal partner is that they refuse to explore other possibilities.

I hate that some women do everything they can to turn men into people they despise.

I hate that women will get angry at men for being direct about their sexual desires while also claiming to hate "the games." You make the rules, we just try to figure them out.

I hate when women get offended that men want sex when their nightstand is packed with fucking dildos.

I hate when women demean men's sexuality, especially masturbation, as gross.

I find it irritating when women think their pussies are so packed with magic fairy dust that they can get away with treating men like shit.

I hate "strong, independent" (™) women who still rely on their pussies to get what they want from men. No, I'm not talking about hookers. I mean ordinary women who threaten men with sexual exile unless the man caves to her demands of the moment.

I hate that nearly every woman reading this has been mentally cataloging a list of "yeah, but" responses. It's a form of deflection that is on the opposite end of attractive.

I hate the number of women reading this who have already decided they don't do any of the above. Yes, you do. Yes, you have. And don't talk to me about honesty until you are introspective enough to admit it.

As you can see, there are aspects of women that I don't like, and yet, I still love women. Keep reading that sentence until it makes sense. Because it totally does.

Far too often women are emotionally stuck in 8th grade. Look at that list and count how many of those things were present in junior high school, and yet remain in play for middle-aged women. 8th grade defined how these women operate in the world, and they have never matured out of it.

Hell, it worked then, right? (Hint: no, it didn't)

I love women enough to want them to be the best they possibly can be. I love them enough to not pretend they are perfect. I love them enough to refuse to participate in their delusions.

I love them enough to hold them to the standards they hold men to, and the ones they hold other women to, and the ones they claim to hold themselves to.

I love them enough to spend a huge amount of effort to try to understand them, how their minds work, and what motivates them to do and say what they do.

It has been said you can't really love something without knowing everything about it. This is so true of men and women. Women often tell me I know more about women than they do themselves. Is that the behavior of a man who hates women?

If any of you still think I fucking hate women, then I am sorry for the personal problems that prevent you from acknowledging or fixing the issues that have impaired your objectivity. But I'm not responsible for your emotional issues and refuse to alter my speech or behaviors to create a fucking safe space for your sorry asses. Grow the fuck up.

Stop fucking blaming men for your problems. Get some fucking help. Take some goddamn responsibility for your stupid fucked-up life. Everyone is a fucking victim in this world. It doesn't make you special. It makes you human.

What is special, what is rare and wonderful, are the women who are emotionally sturdy. It is so fucking attractive you can't possibly imagine.

Let me add one more thing. The list of things above are mostly stuff I've observed but had little-to-no personal experience with. I've been extremely fortunate regarding the amazing women who bless my life.

God, how I love women. Believe it or not.

Why Do Men Love Boobs?

Bewbs. Glorious bewbs.

Has any other body part been the subject of so much discussion, outrage, speculation, attention, and misunderstanding? Besides the clit, I can't think of any.

What's the deal with guys and bewbs, anyway? What are the Roolz? As you might imagine, this is a, um, broad, complicated subject that is a real handful to grasp, and sometimes, er, pendulous and hypnotic and….

[*Back in one moment.* – SK]

[*Did you get it* handled? – Editor]

So… back to the subject.

[*You aren't the only editor in the world.* – SK]

A Brief History of Bewbs

All mammals have mammary glands. Hence the classification name. During estrus, female mammaries become engorged. This is one of the signs that a female is ovulating.

Non-human mammals only have sex during this time. More or less. The males still want it, but the females are not receptive.

Human females are the only species of mammal to have permanently engorged mammary glands (a.k.a. boobs, bewbs, tits, titties, cans, jugs, guns, twin peaks, towers of power, hooters, fun bags, etc. Oh, also breasts. Almost forgot that one!).

Speculation among anthropologists is that bewbs evolved as part of a strategy to keep males around to help provide and protect for their offspring. Women kept their enlarged bewbs all the time and kept the desire for sex outside of ovulation, also to keep the man around.

To a male, bewbs = sex, because nature designed them that way.

The Hunter's Eye

Now factor in that men have single-focus attention, with a keen eye for movement—essential skills when hunting saber-toothed squirrels.

Men can differentiate a female from a male at a quarter mile, given 20/20 vision. No exaggeration. This is important because:

Bewbs = women = sex

This explains why bewbs in motion capture our full attention, almost causing a circuit overload, whether we want it to, or not. It's like a Reese's Peanut Butter Cup. Or, crossing the streams of unlicensed nuclear accelerators. It's simply the genetic wiring.

Radar, Not Lasers

Women have complicated relationships with their bewbs. (Who is surprised by this? Anyone?) They don't want to be defined by them. But they compare theirs to other women. They judge other women by their bewbs, and especially how they are displayed.

Teenage girls can't wait to get them. They want the boys to notice they are getting them. But they don't want to be stared at. Or, more correctly, they don't want them to be stared at by the wrong boys.

Women want to be desired and they learn early their bewbs factor into that equation. What takes longer to learn is that their sexuality broadcasts like radar, and not a laser beam that strikes only the ones they are interested in.

Which is why young men are baffled when a woman puts her tits on display to full advantage, then gets pissy about men looking at them. She wants them to be noticed, just not by him.

Sudden Implant

Why do implants have an impact? Why are women so divided over them?

The women who stand opposed to implants get rather, hmmm, irritated because men are just as attracted (generally speaking) to fake bewbs as real ones. Men are stoopid and superficial, they whine. (Don't like the word whine? How about pout, instead?)

And why do these women even care? I'm getting ahead of myself. One thing at a time.

Here's the simple explanation for why men can't help but notice fake bewbs. It's because our limbic systems do not care if they are fake. This ancient, tiny lizard brain sees bewbs, wants bewbs. It does not notice or care how they came into existence. This section of the brain evolved long before implants, so it has not evolved the capacity to care about the difference.

Some men develop a preference for natural over silicone, but don't think that can shut up the lizard in our heads.

On the other side, a lot of women are horrible to each other. Mean, vicious, and even violent. This is, in my experience, because they view competition as a zero-sum game. That is, one can only win at the expense of others.

These women see implants (and, to a lesser extent, other cosmetic surgeries) as a kind of cheating, and the men who are attracted to them (because nature made us that way) as easily duped morons.

Did I say all women? No. So let it go.

Bewb Roolz For Men

To the eternal frustration of men, women control access to sex. So, given that our brains operate on the formula

Bewbs = women = sex

women also control access to bewbs. Which make sense, since they belong to women. This may seem obvious, but apparently not all guys grasp this simple concept.

Women make the bewb Roolz for men. Naturally, the Roolz are not clearly defined, never documented (until now!), never openly expressed except through anger and scorn, and they have exceptions.

Ignore Them

This is the first, best, and always appropriate rule. Every woman has bewbs. You've seen thousands of them, some covered, some naked, some online, some in person. Don't leer, don't drool, don't comment on them.

Women want to be treated like people, first and foremost. Which leads to the second Rool.

Be Cool

Before NFL Hall of Fame wide receiver Steve Largent caught his first touchdown, he asked one of the veteran players what he should do in the end zone.

He said, "Act like you've been there before, like it's no big deal."

Bewbs are everywhere, attached to every woman. Some are downright spectacular. So what? Act like you've been there before.

Don't Ignore Them

If a woman is flirting with you, and she makes an overt gesture of drawing attention to her girls, take an appreciative look somewhere between a glance and a stare.

Smile at her, look her in the eye and say one single word in response, like "Beautiful." No gimmick lines or sleazy shit. Simply let her know you notice and appreciate her attributes.

Paws Off

It disgusts me that this even needs to be mentioned.

Unless you are in a consensual relationship with a woman, you have no goddamn business touching her bewbs, or any other place. End of discussion.

Never Stare

Research shows when a man looks at a woman, he tends to scan from the feet up. (Women tend to follow the reverse path. Of course.)

This means, you get one free look when you first meet a woman, so long as your gaze does not stop on her bewbs, and you don't take too long doing it. A quick scan is all you get.

Otherwise, it's strictly eye contact. Ahem. By this I mean, when she is looking at you. If she looks away, take another glance, but be quick about it. Don't get caught.

If you do get caught looking? Own it. Look her in the eyes, give a sheepish little smile, a small shrug, and say, "Sorry, but they are very nice."

Always Stare

I have a couple of women friends I can be very open with. From time to time, I have been known to say, "Wait, hold on. I need to look at your bewbs for a minute." They laugh, I look, the conversation goes on. But this is an advanced technique used in unique relationships. Be very careful with this.

The Roolz change completely when a woman wants to have sex. This is when she wants those glorious mounds to be worshiped. Now is the time to show her your appreciation, to tell her how magnificent they are, as part of the whole worship and admiration package deal.

Be aware that every woman has their preferences for the slang terms for breasts. It behooves you to find out which ones she likes and, especially, which ones she hates.

Bewb Roolz For Women

I hope you have a fresh appreciation for how men experience bewbs. You have no idea the willpower it takes a teenage boy to keep from grabbing every tit he sees. That is not a joke or hyperbole. We get used to controlling that urge, but we still feel it.

So, appreciate the efforts of men who show respect to women.

Understand that you don't get to control who is attracted to your body. You broadcast your sexuality in every direction. Just be aware of this and try to be less surprised (and openly disgusted) when unintended men pick up on it. Radar, not lasers.

Appreciate a man who looks but doesn't stare. Try to not get pissy if you do catch him stealing another look, especially if you are wearing something intended to draw attention to your bewbs. He thinks you're beautiful. What's so awful about that?

Men like women who appreciate the beauty in other women without getting jealous. If you ever say, "Do you think she's attractive?" and it's a setup, he will lose significant trust in you. Do not give a man tests. A man of experience and integrity learns to sniff those out. Whether he passes or fails, you will lose.

Instead, say, "Look at the brunette at the bar. Isn't she gorgeous?" That will earn big points with him.

Remember the words of one former Playmate, who said the only thing worse than having men stare at your body is having them not stare.

Men love bewbs. Be glad they do.

Silliness Is Fucking Serious

I couldn't wait until my daughters were old enough to show them *Monty Python and the Holy Grail*. That can't come as much of a surprise by this point.

I really don't remember the actual event so much as the aftermath. My girls and I watched it many times over the years. They could quote entire scenes, and I contributed a line here and there. We had a million laughs with the material.

Their mother felt outside of this daddy-daughter fun. She didn't care for the movie, and it puzzled me. Our daughters were a product of us both, but both girls loved the movie. It wasn't a gender thing.

Now and again, the topic of *Holy Grail* would come up with other adults. Most of the time the couple was also split over their love of the movie.

One time I thought to ask one of the wives how old she was when she first saw it. She was in her twenties. I had been the one to introduce Monty Python to my wife. My daughters had been around 10 and 8.

When one woman who loved the movie revealed she had also seen it as young girl, the idea clicked that age was a factor. Perhaps it was the factor.

Thus, I began a decades-long informal survey of women regarding *Holy Grail*. Whenever the subject of the movie came up in conversation (and it actually does), I asked any women present how old they were when they first saw it, and if they liked it.

A clear dividing line emerged, age-wise: 18. Younger, and girls love it, but once that magic number is reached, then not much, if at all.

As if to prove this theory, one friend saw *Holy Grail* two months before her eighteenth birthday. She's ambivalent towards the movie. She was on the cusp, in the middle of whatever transition takes place.

The next question to emerge was why this is the case. I didn't put much thought into this aspect until a few weeks ago when I was asked a very important question.

"Why?"

I had no idea.

Clearly women who don't like *Holy Grail* can still have a sense of humor. What happens to a young woman at that specific age, what changes in her, to make her unable to appreciate the ridiculous nonsense of Monty Python?

The answer lies within the movie itself, in a famous line from King Arthur (yes, I know, they are all famous).

On second thought, let's not go to Camelot. It is a silly place.

The whole thing is a silly place! It's a silly movie, start to finish!

When girls become adult women, they abandon silliness. Or lose it. Something happens that kills their child-like silliness. And it happens during a shockingly small window of time.

This loss is manifest in the battle cry of The Serious Woman, "Well, somebody has to be the adult!"

In the case of mothers, there is the additional theme directed at the dads, "I wish I had time to get on the floor and play with the kids." Why don't they? Because play is silly, and their ability to be silly has been rooted out.

The good news is that, for reasons I cannot yet explain, watching *Holy Grail* at a young age helps girls preserve (at least) some of their silliness into adulthood. These women can be serious adults but also silly, as they choose. They have options.

Do men experience the same thing? Perhaps, but not to the same extent. Men seem more capable of hanging onto some of their silliness into adulthood.

Or maybe they just have all seen *Holy Grail* as boys.

There is a vast difference between silliness and funny. Silly is an attitude. Silly is what little children do. They make faces, they see dragons in the forest, they burp and fart and laugh at all of it.

Funny is a skill that takes a lot of time plus trial and error to perfect. And I'm not even counting the people who try to be professionals at it.

Lots of people try to be funny when they aren't. This is particularly true of men. Just because you find something funny does not mean others will. You know damn well what I'm talking about. You remember telling an anecdote or joke and the group fell deadly silent afterward.

So, recover your childish silliness and leave the funny shit to people who can pull it off.

Ending the Hurts

BECAUSE THAT'S WHAT IT WOULD MEAN IF I DID IT.

Remember these words. Repeat them often until they become a part of you. They will change your life and your relationships for the better.

Now I will explain. It's so terrifyingly simple you may not embrace the truth.

When somebody does or says something that hurts, we apply our own meaning to the words or action. It hurts because that's what it would mean if we did it.

We don't even consider the possibility that the other person has their own experiences and meanings. We instantly apply our meaning to them. When it's a bad meaning, we get hurt, because that's what it would mean if we did it.

Forgetting my birthday means she doesn't love me, because that's what it would mean if I did it.

We also apply an unintended good meaning to words or actions.

Touching my arm means she likes me, because that's what it would mean if I did it.

There's a sneaky, tricky tactic for discovering the other person's meaning. It's complicated, so pay attention to all the steps and don't leave any out.

1. Ask.

If you don't want to follow those steps, then just let go of the imagined hurt. Which is a good idea anyway.

Here is a fun drinking game (if you hate your liver and your life). It goes like this: whenever you hear/read of someone explaining the motivations behind the words and/or actions of another, insert this phrase at the end of each sentence:

...BECAUSE THAT'S WHAT IT WOULD MEAN IF I DID IT.

Of course, you and I would never do something like that. We understand that other people are motivated by reasons and experiences different from our own, and we can't know what they are without asking.

Lena Dunham provides a Real-Life (Minor Celebrity Edition) example of this kind of thinking.

> "I was sitting next to Odell Beckham Jr., and it was so amazing because it was like he looked at me and he determined I was not the shape of a woman by his standards [*because that's what it would mean if I did it*]," she said. "He was like, 'That's a marshmallow. That's a child. That's a dog.'[*Because that's what it would mean if I did it.*] It wasn't mean—he just seemed confused, [*because that's what it would mean if I did it.*]"

This is why you don't want to make it a drinking game. You'd be over the legal limit after one Dunham paragraph.

It also exposes more about the speaker than the person spoken about, usually highly unflattering things.

If you want to stop this behavior in yourself, it starts with spotting it in others. It will help develop an awareness of how pervasive this thinking is. Asking is hard, scary, risky. Assuming is easy.

Always remember these words.

BECAUSE THAT'S WHAT IT WOULD MEAN IF I DID IT.

Your Credibility Rating

I sat down for the latest round of Project Cleanup, wherein I list all my unfinished projects as a starting point for clearing some of them away. Ever do that? I know people who would require pages to list their started but incomplete projects.

Let's be honest. Starting is fun. Finishing is hard. I've been forced to learn finishing via my primary vocation. If you are lucky enough to work in a deadline-driven industry, then you have been drafted into the Finisher's Reserves. A surprising number of people never learn the skill of wrapping up a project.

Still, I have unfinished projects. An interview that needs to be transformed into an article, two art projects, a bedroom that is partially painted. You get the idea.

Finishing a project provides a huge emotional response, even if the project is no more inspiring than to keep the blackberries from taking over (more of) the back yard. Finishing is a relief, a release. I can't finish a project without a monster-sized sigh of relief.

Here's why.

Projects Are Debt

Accepting a new project means you have committed into the future your most valuable resource, your time, towards the completion of the project. Being that this is a project and not just a task, it cannot be completed in a single sitting. Therefore, your time has become encumbered by the liability of the project. Does it matter if a project is just for you? No, it does not, not in the sense of whether the project incurs time-debt.

If you buy a model airplane for yourself, you've accepted that project, even if you never open the box. Taking the smallest step towards a project implies accepting the whole project, or at a minimum your roll in the project. Don't buy the fabric or the yarn, or the lumber or the tools, for a project until you are also ready to accept the debt-load of accepting the project. Don't tell your buddy or parents or children you are going to do a project until you are ready to finish it.

When it comes to project debt the only "someday" projects are the ones you haven't begun at all.

How "Interesting" Becomes Interest

There is a carrying cost for unfinished projects. Let's call it interest on the debt. I accepted the project of painting a bedroom. But, let's say I did that to put off doing the painting, reasoning that committing would buy me a few weeks of peace on the subject.

The problem is my brain is now required to track the project. It knows I have committed to it and that I'm not working on it. It costs attention and energy even if I never take a single step beyond the verbal commitment. Every day a project remains incomplete is another day of paying interest.

In addition, the time that has been reserved to painting can't be committed to other projects in the same timeframe. You can't (responsibly—see below) sell the same time to more than one "buyer" so, while the painting project sits unfinished and perhaps barely started, it is tying up mental and physical capacity for no purpose except carrying costs.

Your Credibility Rating

That isn't to say people can't and don't work on multiple concurrent projects. Of course they do, and it is OK, if you take care of your credibility rating.

Have you ever known people who commit to projects at the drop of a hat but rarely, if ever, complete them? Just like financial bankruptcy, time bankruptcy is ruinous. Taking on more projects than you have time to work on leads to defaults, missed "payments" of project deliverables, all of which causes a downgrade in your credibility. Even, or especially, with yourself.

Overspending your ability to repay leads to a damaged credit rating and, if unchecked, bankruptcy.

Overspending your time does the same to your credibility, your reputation. The people who track your credibility rating are your friends, family, and coworkers. We all do it. We don't want to work with, or for, a credibility bankrupt.

Clearing Debt

There is only one way to clear project debt. No, two ways. There are only two ways to clear project debt. Wait, there's a third. OK, there are only three (I'm sure it is only three) ways to remove project debt from your personal ledger.

Finish it! Seems obvious, but I know people for whom it might come as a shock. Have you noticed how good it feels to put in some work on a project and see it move forward, even a little bit? That's because your debt-load has gone down a bit, and your interest payments are also decreased. Great feeling, right?

Quit! Yes, you can often simply decide to no longer participate in a project. But you must take some concrete steps. If others are involved, you must tell them and do a responsible hand-off regarding the state of the project to those who remain with it. If it is personal and does not involve others, then clear away the detritus of the commitment. Throw away the partially completed items. Donate what can be donated. Clear it out! You are done with the project, you've quit it, so clear it away and don't look back.

Renegotiate! See if you can change the terms of your time commitment. Instead of working 10 hours a week on that Algebra text, perhaps 4 hours is more realistic. Maybe you can delay painting the living room until June? You'll have to get other parties to agree if this is more than a personal project, but they might if you can make a reasonable case. You'll still carry the debt and pay the interest, but renegotiating terms can keep you out of bankruptcy.

Delegate it! (Ok, five—no four—ways.) If you can get away with having somebody else do the work, then you can increase your time-capacity by using their time.

If you feel tired and overwhelmed, consider the possibility that your project debt load is at or over your limit. Use the options above to clear away some project debt and feel the surge of energy. I know I do.

Part III: Palette Cleansers

The Blurb That Wasn't

Ask any author about their least favorite writing task and, more often than not, they will surround the word 'blurb' with a fuck-load of curse words. When I could procrastinate the task no longer, I poured a glass of whiskey and cut loose with whatever came to mind.

When it was presented to a group of authors for feedback, a dividing line grew stark. Some didn't get it at all but the ones who got it, they really got it. Nobody straddled the fence. They loved it or hated it.

I came to think of it as a tribal test. As much as I liked that notion, it simply was too harsh for everyone. The next night, after more whiskey, I wrote two more editions, eventually selecting the third for General Audiences.

Here is the first version. You'll know in a flash which side of the line you fall on.

You've sensed it, felt it, but haven't dared to acknowledge it even in the darkest moments of the night. You're not like everyone else.

You a horrible person.

There's chance you're right, of course, but come on. Nobody truly horrible spends one second worrying about it.

Know why the same shit keeps happening to you? Because you keep doing the same shit without thinking about why, or what the effects are, or anything, really. You wander around like a robotic parrot, um, parroting the same words, thoughts, ideas that you've always, er, parroted.

You have no idea how many things you do but fail to think about, and the mess those things make out of your life. You drag yourself through one disaster after another, asking yourself, "Why does this shit always happen to me?"

Until now.

I mean, not exactly right now, because you have to buy the book, and start reading it. But then! Then you will finally begin to grasp the enormity of the vast empty space of your mind.

OK, that didn't come out right.

Just open the book, OK? Find out about (some of) the things I have wasted my life thinking about because nobody else has bothered. You could have done it and saved me the time, but no.

Thanks for nothing.

What Are Daily-ish Horoscopes?

Here's what I believe regarding Astrology. Not that you care, and I'm not trying to convince anyone. This is simply an explanation. Got it?

I think Nurse Jackson and the doctor playing Johnny Bench to your slippery hide had a far stronger gravitational influence on you at birth than do other planets. For that matter, why isn't everybody's sign "Mom" because her gravity surrounded you for 9 months?

But I'm not militant about it. I know my sign. I've had my natal chart done. Hell, I've consulted with psychics. For me, it's entertainment.

One day on Facebook, someone posted some kind of horoscope and I thought, "Dude, we could totally make up shit like that, only maybe it would be funny."

And so it began.

I quickly modified the title to "Daily-ish" so I wouldn't be obligated to come up with something every damn day. Plus, on a few days I've posted more than one. Hence, the -ish part.

Maybe you will enjoy them, maybe you won't.

Maybe it's up to the stars.

The Horoscopes

FEBRUARY 2018

2018.02.04
Send me $99 and you'll find love and good fortune.

Oh, that's my horoscope.

2018.02.20
You know that person you've been thinking about? Stop it.

2018.02.21
It's worse than you thought.

2018.02.22
Don't chose that one, take the other one. No, to the right... a little... there.

2018.02.23
A free-for-all is not, in fact, free.

2018.02.23
You can tell how boring a movie will be from trailer music.

2018.02.25
Do you turn frogs into princes, or princes into frogs?

2018.02.25
Get serious about being silly. What the fuck are you waiting for?

2018.02.26
Test your feelings against physics and see which wins. Go on. I'll wait.

2018.02.28
100% of your problems are caused by your shitty self-worth

MARCH 2018

2018.03.02
Nature can be so beautiful that it's easy to forget it wants to kill you.

2018.03.02
STFU about politics. You will never convince anyone. Save that shit for family dinner.

2018.03.03
Some of the best things in life are cheese

2018.03.04
It's not your fault the lottery keeps getting the numbers wrong

2018.03.08
Authenticity is the new Pickup Artist.

2018.03.11
You're on your own. Don't act like this was a surprise.

2018.03.13
Remember, the earth itself is bipolar.

2018.03.13
Dance like train wreck. Of course people are going to watch so give them a show to remember.

2018.03.14
Thursday is the worst. Not humpday, not yet Friday. The wallflower of the week.

2018.03.15
Be judgmental and discriminatory. Judge who makes you better. Show discrimination in who you let into your life.

2018.03.19
You started it. Stop with the fingers, you know you did.

2018.03.21
Forgetfulness Awareness Day was yesterday. I think we have it nailed.

2018.03.23
You can't have worse timing than me and still be alive. So, you have that going for you.

APRIL 2018

2018.04.05
The thing you are unwilling to do is the thing you will be required to do.

2018.04.06
A thing not worth doing at all is not worth doing well.

2018.04.11
You can lead a person to knowledge, but you can't make them think.

2018.04.12
It's National Grilled Cheese day. Or, at my house, Thursday.

2018.04.14
Breakfast for dinner, because you are the boss of you.

2018.04.15
Being alone and being lonely are not the same thing.

2018.04.16
What if we create, promote, or allow everything that happens to us?

2018.04.19
Authenticity is the new Spanish Fly. Except it actually works.

2018.04.19
I had something for this. It was really good.

2018.04.22
The world is full of Dr. Leo Marvins. Dare to be a Bob Wiley.

2018.04.22
It's Lenin's birthday. He accidentally murdered millions. Could happen to anyone.

2018.04.23
Whatever you decide never go half-assed. Always go fully assed.

2018.04.23
The world has sadly not ended. The bank still wants to be paid.

2018.04.24
Women tell each other they are queens but nobody is teaching them how to keep a king.

2018.04.26
Whatever you want to be better at, practice it. Practice isn't just for music and sport. It's for everything.

2018.04.27
You're pretty great. Most of the time. Er, sometimes. I mean, you're tolerable on occasion.

2018.04.27
Mature is how I behave. Immature is how you behave. So there!

2018.04.29
I can overthink you under the table.

2018.04.30
Since the female orgasm is like 90% mental, a man is little more than a tour guide.

MAY 2018

2018.05.01
The worst thing you can do to a person is give them exactly what they say they want.

2018.05.01
Being broke is a state of finances. Being poor is a state of mind.

2018.05.02
Strength of courage is proportional to the distance from the danger.

2018.05.04
Like yesterday but with more water.

2018.05.07
Have a lovely Tues... wait, what day is it?

2018.05.08
Yes, you are paranoid. But, you're also being watched. Good luck sorting that out.

2018.05.09
If you take all the marbles nobody can play with you.

2018.05.10
The sun may well come out tomorrow but what about today? Does it have another solar system on the side?

2018.05.10
Half & Half should be called One.

2018.05.14
"You only live once." And people call ME cynical?

2018.05.14
When it looks like you are facing a contradiction, check your premises. At least one of them will be wrong.

2018.05.15
Words are the musical notes of our thoughts.

2018.05.15
Your better judgment has given up even trying.

2018.05.15
Did you ever expect to spend so much of your life clicking, the 'turn off notifications' button?

2018.05.16
No good idea is safe from being ruined by zealots.

2018.05.18
Days are neither good nor bad, they are just blocks of time. People fuck that shit up. Don't blame time.

2018.05.18
You were born under the sign of Nurse Kelly. It's a rare privilege but she did have quite a bit of gravity.

2018.05.21
Tomorrow is promised to no one. But options are available on a limited basis.

2018.05.22
Dogs don't have boogers.

2018.05.23
Better get that looked at. You can probably find volunteers.

2018.05.24
Some people get a lot of satisfaction by eliminating every drop of joy from life. Keep them far away.

2018.05.28
OK: imaginary friends. Better: imaginary stripper friends.

2018.05.29
The irony is that the anonymity of the Internet reveals who a person truly is.
Ah, shit.

2018.05.29
One key appeal of any hobby is the gear. No wonder so many cyclists are assholes.

2018.05.30
It's Wednesday, motherfuckers! See if you can raise your enthusiasm to apathy levels.

2018.05.30
As summer approaches, my friends, remember that "under the cover of darkness" becomes shorter and shorter.

JUNE 2018

2018.06.01
The Universe is tired of people putting words in its mouth.

2018.06.02
Imagine growing up with the name Benedict Cumberbatch. I bet he's a tough motherfucker.

2018.06.03
Maple syrup is tree blood.

2018.06.05
Don't like negative energy? Just try living without electrons, motherfuckers. Don't give me no static.

2018.06.05
The Law of Diminishing Returns does not apply to pepperoni.

2018.06.07
Don't 'should' on yourself and don't 'should' on others. 'Should' is the express bus from reality to crazy town.

2018.06.07
Do not ever say, "Things can't get any worse." Unless you enjoy being wrong on an epic scale.

2018.06.11
Try to limit yourself to one Monday a week.

2018.06.12
Walking through the open doors will change your life.
Walking into closed doors will get you into treatment.

2018.06.14
The little things are the big things.

2018.06.14
Success in life often comes down to remembering your point while still speaking. We are all fucked.

2018.06.15
Drinking alone may be a sign you have a problem. So, get a dog. Or a cactus.

2018.06.17
Every fear is the fear of some kind of pain.

2018.06.18
It's too hot to take over the world today. Stay inside and color.

2018.06.19
When someone asks, "Do you want me to be completely honest?" Just say no.

2018.06.19
Even if you are God, your circle of friends is not the whole world.

2018.06.19
The more people panic over something the more likely they are to be wrong. You're welcome.

2017.06.21
Men are no good... at behaving like women. And why would you want them to? Women already got that covered.

2017.06.21
Avoid sending mixed messages. Like, "Have fun, be safe."

2018.06.24
Do you ever wonder how much pet hair you eat in a week? Well, you do now.

2018.06.27
Auntie Em was kind of a bitch. Maybe we didn't see her at her best. Then again, maybe we did.

2018.06.28
Respect can't be demanded, it has to be earned. Especially by blood.

2018.06.28
Getting old and getting older are not at all the same.

2018.06.28
The clothes basket is getting low. Time to do laundry.

JULY 2018

2018.07.03
Everything comes at a cost and the price of love is pain. It's an investment, really.

2018.07.04
The sole purpose of some people is to introduce you to others you need to meet.

2018.07.04
Things that have never happened before happen all the time.

2018.07.05
Things do happen for a reason. Often the reason is someone is a dumb shit.

2018.07.06
Don't think of it as being out of shape. Think of it as having morphed into a new shape.

2018.07.06
Stop crying about life being unfair. Life never made that promise and you sound like a fucking toddler.

2018.07.11
It's high time you did something about your pathetic self-worth, you stupid freak.

2018.07.13
"The best defense is a good offense." It works for war, and it works for driving.

2018.07.15
Honey butter > honey and butter. Explain that one.

2018.07.16
Just because it's your dream and your passion doesn't mean you'll be any good at it.

2018.07.17
Make being amazing look easy. Or, just be amazing at easy things.

2018.07.18
Everything you want is on the other side of Xanax.

The Recovery Session

The stubby woman with rebellious hair strode to the front of the room. People slumped in various chairs, some with sunglasses on, others holding their heads as if to keep them from fracturing. To her left stood a pair of stern EMTs.

"Welcome to Berit Recovery," said Grace Quillen in her Lauren Bacall voice. She turned to a small table, picking up a glass of Maker's Mark and a joint.

"One sec," she muttered while flicking a lighter. A long drag, then a longer hold, then an extended coughing fit.

"Whew! That's some good shit," she said, chasing the hit with the whiskey.

"Who wants some?" Hands went up all around the room. "Jesus, you people are dumbass suckers. This is mine. You are addicts. You can't handle this shit. Morons."

Grace poured another drink. "I am here to help you pathetic people get over your stupid addictions to your ex's and crushes, and all the relationships, real or imagined, that you simply refuse to get over."

After knocking back the drink, Grace said, "We have a simple philosophy here at Berit Recovery. Which I will demonstrate now."

"You, what is your deal?" she said, pointing at a young woman in the first row.

The woman looked around, nervously. "It's my boyfriend. Ex-boyfriend. We were—"

"Nobody cares, sweetie," said Grace. "Do you want to get over him?"

The woman nodded.

"Who else would like to be done with their addiction to the people who don't love them?"

All hands go up.

Grace picked up a rubber mallet, walked to the woman in the first row, and smashed her kneecap. She screamed in pain while the EMTs assisted her out of the room.

Waving the mallet, Grace asks, "Anyone else? No? Then get out of here. You're cured."

Part IV: Relationships Suck

Fucking Kiss Her Like A Man

[*Like a man would. Not like she's a man. Let's be clear on this point.* – SK]

I pulled back from delivering what I hoped was the deal-sealing kiss.

"You do know how to kiss. You could just refine it."

I laughed. Know how? Fucking know how? Refine it...how?

I know how to kiss and have the blue ribbons to prove it.

[*There are no ribbons* – Editor]

[*If ribbons could be won for kissing, I'd have them. Which I do. Totally do. Also, shut up.* – SK]

People don't kiss anymore, not like they used to so, why should I care?

Which is exactly the point. Women complain that men have forgotten how to kiss a woman properly. Let me tell you, brothers, they love to be expertly kissed, yet too many men would have to work hard to be mediocre.

[*Not a single blue ribbon among them* – SK]

[*It's not a thing* – Ed.]

Before getting into the mechanics of a great kiss, you need to know why it matters. There are two key points as to why you guys need to shape up and learn how to fucking kiss her.

Why It Fucking Matters to Her

Don't take my word for it. I asked three women, let's call them Bella, Ellen, and Lara, to throw back the curtain on the female mind on the subject of kissing.

First, women have thought about the subject of a truly great kiss. A lot. They can describe the perfect kiss the way you can look at a rusted out '56 Belle Aire and know what it could be when restored.

And you know, if a woman puts that much mental energy into something, it matters to her.

Second, you know how a woman will say, for example, leaving socks on the floor means you don't love her? They affix meaning to everything and kissing has far more meaning than even I imagined.

Ellen said, "[Kissing] matters because it can tell you a lot about how an individual is going to function in a relationship. Great kisses make it hard to walk or even stand up."

"A great kiss is like a whisper in the ear that the other person knows you, yet yearns to know your nuances more completely," said Lara. "It is intimate to gaze into another's eyes and connect before and during kissing. It is an indicator of how sex will be."

Women need to feel a connection before having sex. Expert-level kissing builds that connection.

Bella said, "It tells us what kind of a man he is. Is he giving? Loving and caring? Or is he forceful or overbearing? If a man is self-assured, not arrogant, women will know it. They will want more. And it also shows what might be to come."

A great kiss is not just physical foreplay for women, but emotional foreplay as well. They believe the kiss is a window to our souls, our character. You can either try to change this long-held belief (you won't), or you can work with it.

Why It Fucking Matters to You

Guys are dumber than a bag made of hair full of doorknobs made of hair, stuffed with more hair. I'm not even kidding.

Every single fucking time you are asked to do something that has been labeled as "a girl thing" you start looking like you've been riding out a six-day typhoon in a dingy. Morons.

Sex is a girl thing you want to do. With girls. Well, there is more involved than putting your little Play-Doh dick into her pussy. You're reading this because you know it, but you don't *really* know it. Some lonely, abandoned neuron has been trying to get your attention on this subject for most of your life. Poor little thing!

In fact, I should thank you for being so squeamish, though. In 9th grade, I had the chance to participate in a revue-type performing group. Singing and dancing. As is always the case, the girls outnumbered the boys 3:1.

Think about that little statistic, you idiots. Three-to-fucking-one. What would you give for those odds now?

And it wasn't just being around them. It was dancing with them. Often very close. While they wore leotards. Plus practices. Plus shows. Plus backstage costume changes.

So, when the tree-necked gorillas tried to mock me for dancing with girls, I responded with, "I was practicing stage kisses while you were rubbing up against other sweaty guys. Which of those things sounds more gay?"

And then I ran as fast as my Capezio's would carry me.

Thanks, you guys, for letting me have those girls to myself.

Jesus. You're still doing that shit, aren't you?

Highway to The Friend Zone

Your poor little pea-brains are probably exhausted by now, so let's keep this short.

There is a way to keep your ass out of the Friend Zone. One. The rule is brutally simple.

1. Friends don't kiss.

Got it? End of story. Unless you kiss her, early and often, and kiss the fucking hell out of her, you are booked on a one-way trip to the Friend Zone.

Do you want more sex? Wait, let me rephrase that. You want more sex. Then become a master at the art of the kiss. Don't believe me? Ask around.

Or is that a girl thing, too?

How to Fucking Kiss Her

Now I'm going to give you the formula for the perfect kiss that works every time with every woman.

Jesus, you are suckers.

If you believe such a thing exists, then you have moved into your own private reality with your own little Unabomber shack. God, it must be lonely there without women.

We will never be able to comprehend, except in very small ways, what women experience in their minds. It isn't apples and oranges, it's apples and lava. The things we imagine will work with women are nearly always wrong, except by accident. Not because all of us are stupid, but because we can't begin to know how their brains function. Yes, it works both ways, and completely not the point.

We guess wrong so fucking often that when we do hit on something that works, we keep pushing that same button over and over until you can't read the writing on it anymore.

Besides, women are like the weather. What worked yesterday may not work ever again, and what we thought was a disaster an hour ago may be exactly what she wants now. Yes, you are totally screwed and not in the fun way.

Being a great kisser is like leading a Tango. Leading isn't controlling, it isn't demanding, it isn't dominating. Leading is about letting the woman know your intentions with small, but clear, indications. She can follow or not. Take a step, see if she follows.

Bella says, "A great kiss in my mind starts with a few pecks then opening your eyes to see what your partner is feeling. If you see that look in their eyes, take it to a deeper kiss. Still no tongue.

Never too much pressure on their lips. You want to let them know you are in control and not a pile of jelly. But that you're interested."

Lara agrees about eye contact, "I like to feel the small smile of delight and open my eyes to see one's eyes, happy that they are with me and holding the knowledge that I am enjoying myself completely."

"So, a great kiss begins with those meaningful glances, that eye contact, preferably even a caress. Chemistry is important," said Ellen.

Pay attention here, men. Eye contact is essential to forming that all-important connection. Plus, for us it's like taking a hit of cocaine. I mean, the exact same parts of the brain get lit up when a woman looks us straight in the eye. So, look her in the eye and ride that high.

The next part is trickier because it varies from person to person, and variation is the name of the game at this stage. Please remember: kissing isn't just for the lips.

Now I'm going to get out of the way and let the women speak.

Ellen: Place is important because while obviously the main goal is mouth-to-mouth contact, there's nothing nicer than trailing kisses from the neck or shoulder first. Taking a quick break to kiss other things, like ears or…whatever, works as well.

Lara: Personally, I like the teasing kiss … firm-ish lips … with a touch of a playful tongue.

Ellen: It's easy to get caught up and stuck on what you like. But your partner might prefer something else or at least like different things at different times.

Bella: Hold off a bit to find out if she wants more. Let her know you want more (if you do) by showing it in your eyes, the quickness of your breath. But not the fierceness of your kiss. That can ruin a good kiss. Like too much movement can frighten off a bird.

Ellen: When I say variety, I mean the pace AND the place. It's nice to vary the intensity from gentle and slow to extremely passionate or maybe the reverse.

Bella: The eyes and breath tell you if she wants more. If she does...the peck deepens. Not attacking by any means, but more lip contact, a soft hand at the base of the neck. Never making her feel trapped but making her want to find out what else you have.

    The good news is that improving at kissing will yield huge benefits, and the practicing ain't bad, either. Plus, women love to kiss, so you won't be getting much resistance.

    Bella gets the final say on this subject.

    "A good kiss is almost as good as the act of sex."

[*No, really, I have ribbons. And trophies.* – SK]
[*Still not a thing.* – Ed.]

Toilet Seat Wars

The war over toilet seats is over. Women have won total victory.

But they have no idea what this meaningless battle has cost them. Nor do they seem to care.

Since the first outhouse, women have insisted, sometimes with great anger, that the seat be put down after the household males take a pee. This is so the women don't fall into the crapper.

This is such a visceral issue that women don't even bother to think about it. But I'm going to, and I will explain why women have lost far more than they gained by winning this debate.

The issue isn't toilet seats. That is just the battleground.

What is up for grabs is respect, responsibility, independence, and sexual objectification. Women have traded all those things to keep their asses dry in the dark.

Everybody has dunked their bits in the chilly waters of the toilet bowl after stumbling, bleary-eyed, into the bathroom in the middle of the night and failing to check the state of the seat. It is an experience we would really prefer to not repeat, male or female.

What goes through a young male's mind at that moment is, "I won't let that happen again!"

What goes through the mind of a young female is figuring out who to blame. The list may be long, or it may be short, but one thing is certain: she is not on it.

Thus, begins a lifelong quest to force every male on earth to take responsibility for what happens to her ass in the middle of the night. She feels righteous indignation over this noble struggle.

She will do anything to win.

Eventually, she does.

And by doing so she loses. Let me count the ways.

Women who one minute decry sexual objectification will in the next minute threaten a permanent sexual famine unless, and until, the damn toilet seat is managed to her specifications.

Women who will demand equality in all things will, at the same time, insist that men are responsible for their own lack of attention over where they put their asses.

Women who insist they can be as rational as any man will lose their shit if their cheeks hit the water in the bowl.

Women who post endless memes about irresponsible men never accept their own part in keeping their own asses dry.

Women who are quick to find sexism lurking behind every gesture nonetheless demand that men manage the state of all toilet seats in perpetuity.

Women use guilt, shame, belittling, threats, anger, and denial of sex to get men to put the damn seat down. Most men acquiesce, sooner or later, but only to achieve a measure of peace. We just don't care the same way you do.

However, there is a better way, ladies. You can win at this without losing anything.

The first thing is to promise yourself to never again blame anyone but yourself for sitting down without checking the toilet seat. And... I lost most of you on that point. For the few still reading, I will explain how to get men to put the seat (and lid) down after each use.

It starts by understanding that men are wired to provide and protect. We can't help it. You can use (or even abuse) this to your benefit.

Find a time when he is not mentally engaged in something. This is important! Do not interrupt him. Especially to say, "We need to talk." Jesus, not ever.

Then phrase your request in terms of what it will provide for you -- and do not say that you are incapable of checking for yourself.

For example:

"Honey, you know how much I love our home, and all we do to make it the best home it can be. I take a lot of pride in our home. When the toilet seat is left up, it takes away from that pride. It's also unhealthy to flush with the lid up. If you would do your best to put the lid down after you use the toilet, it would make our home healthier, and it will help me feel better about living here."

Use your own words, of course. The point is to give him the chance to do something for you for reasons he can grok.

Follow up by putting a little thank you note on the lid the first few times he remembers, to reinforce your appreciation. He won't be perfect for quite a while so patience is required. No scolding.

Simply reiterate the previous conversation, but with praise for the progress and a kind request for the improvement to continue.

You can get what you want, keep your sanity, and let your man have a win as well. He needs that, you know. Or you should by now.

The Most Common Denominator

It's late on Sunday night. I've had a solid nightcap, and I'm writing this on my phone. Let's see how this turns out, eh? Should be interesting!

Ready?

I can tell you exactly what's wrong with your dating, with your relationships.

But you really don't want to know the answer. You should probably stop reading now. No, really. Go away. You won't like this one bit, and that cracks me the hell up!

Ok, I warned you.

Think about the people you have dated. Think about the relationships. All of them. Not just the horrible ones. Not just the romantic ones. Friends, too. Not family, because you didn't choose them. Stop with the metaphysics shit. You didn't choose your family.

What do all these people have in common? You.

Told you so. You don't want that to be the answer. Not that. Anything but that!

Mommy and Daddy said you were special. You were their perfect little angel. Clearly, *you* could not ever be the problem, so you wield the blame-thrower like a firehose. It's all them, all their fault. Stupid assholes. Fucking bitches.

Except the same shit keeps happening. Every fucking time. Which means it's you. Don't worry, it's me, too.

There was a moment last winter when my thinking shifted from

"Why are all the women who are attracted to me so broken?"

to

"Why am I only attracting broken women?"

Do you see the difference? No, not the number of words! Do you see how the formulation of the question can lead to different answers? Squint if you need to.

Asking a different question is when it became clear. I was the common denominator.

We keep playing out the same stupid patterns, attracting the same stupid kinds of people, failing the same stupid ways. Pointing our same stupid fingers at everyone but our own stupid selves.

The only way to get a different result in our relationships is to become a different person. That's fancy talk for changing. It's brutally hard to see ourselves clearly, without becoming defensive, and to take deliberate steps to grow. It can be terrifying.

So what? For fuck's sake, you aren't in diapers anymore. Or again.

If you're not going to grow the duck up, [*A little autocorrect humor.* – SK] [*Very ducking little.* – Editor] get off your ass and figure out what changes you need to make, then shut up about how you can't find the one you're wishing for.

Either way, stop with the whining and moaning and complaining. Stop pointing fingers. Stop all that fucking shit. It's unattractive, so you know.

Someone who is making serious progress on themselves is attractive. Someone who takes responsibility for what happens in their relationships is smoking hot.

Do the work. Study. Think. Contemplate. Grow. Lather. Rinse. Repeat. Until you die.

Because if nothing changes, then nothing fucking changes.

That's all. Goodnight.

Online Relationships Are an Illusion

If you are old enough to have seen Star Wars (when there was only one) in the theaters, I bet you remember the moment when the entire audience fell in love with R2D2.

You know what I'm talking about. It's when he gets zapped, screams, and falls over.

R2D2 had already presented as a likable character, even while speaking no words the audience could understand. But the zapping sealed the deal with everyone.

Without looking, how far into the movie would you say that scene took place? (Originally. Not accounting for "enhanced" editions.)

Eight minutes.

Most of that time was not spent on R2D2 and C3PO, which is important to this essay.

I'm going to talk about the perception of time, and how it relates to stories and characters but also relationships—online and in real life—and why this can be disorienting to women especially.

For example, have you ever had this kind of conversation, or thought it yourself?

"Remember last year when we started texting each other?"

"It was six weeks ago."

Why does an online relationship (of any kind) so often feel like it has been going on much longer than the calendar will admit to? What does this have to do with R2D2? And do I have to get zapped?

To answer the last first, you might get zapped sooner than you would in real life. So be ready.

Many years ago, researchers did one of those "duh" surveys that everyone already knows the answer to. The asked which co-worker you would feel closer to: one you worked with 40 hours one week or one you worked with one hour a week for 40 weeks?

Almost everyone picked the second coworker, because they had "known them longer." It was the same amount of time together, just spread out differently. But this is the first clue to the puzzle.

We perceive length of relationships through the lens of time using two factors: overall number of hours, and days.

Although this seems to argue against the distortion of time in online relationships, it provides the key to both R2D2 and the hot guy/girl you are chasing. I mean, opening up a meaningful dialog with.

The key to understanding both R2D2 and the object of your online affections is editing. More precisely, the effects of editing.

If you take all of the shots with R2D2 in them and splice the together, you suddenly discover that a) it's not very much screen time, and b) the emotional impact of the zap is almost zero.

Why? Because you don't feel like you spent enough time with the character. How does a few minutes of other shots cause us to feel closer to R2D2?

Just because I need a term for this, I will call it connection disruption, but that might change. It will do for now.

Every time there is a cut from R2D2 to other action taking place with other characters, another connection disruption occurs. That is, the connection between the audience and R2D2. Our minds insert a perceptual time gap after each disruption.

This makes it feel like R2D2 is the one hour a week coworker instead of the one-week coworker.

With all the cuts to other action, by the time R2D2 gets zapped, we feel a connection with him which is sealed by his human-like reaction.

"But," you may argue. "There's no editor in a text conversation!" It's a completely understandable position.

And completely wrong.

A text conversation isn't a phone call. There is almost always a gap between text messages. Those are cuts! Plus, we have life going on around us at the same time.

Everything that pulls our attention from texting creates yet another edit-like cut.

An hour texting can build the perception of a very long time spent talking. An hour a day for a week can feel like months.

Compare that to a long evening conversing with a friend. Hours pass, and it feels like minutes because there were no edits. No disruptions to the connection.

The online perception is a distortion of reality our brains invent without our permission or knowledge. It is an artifact of the technology. It isn't deliberate the way film editing is.

Going back to the temp workers earlier, the number of connection disruptions (all else being equal) is 5 for the one-week person versus 40 for the other. Viewed this way, it's easy to understand why the second feels like a stronger bond.

I believe this perception distortion adversely affects women more than men, and men need to be aware of this.

Time is the cruel overlord of women. From the unrelenting ticking of the "biological clock" to how aging affects them sooner, and more so than men.

Women tend to have an unconscious set of time guidelines for how a relationship should progress. Even though most are unaware of it, this timeline leaks out in conversations.

"Why aren't you [moving in together, engaged, exclusive, etc.] yet? It's been [x] months/years already?" That's the timeline speaking. There are acceptable upper and lower boundaries to each stage of a relationship.

The reason for the timeline is because women need to know when to bail on a relationship, and the sooner the better, so they can find a mate who will stick with them. Even if women don't want to get married. Even if they don't want kids. The timeline rules the progress of relationships.

Of course, not every woman is guided by a timeline. Add in whatever other disclaimers make you happy. The fact is, many women operate relationships based on their internal timelines.

What happens when the timeline calendar and the distortion from an online relationship collide? Disorientation, insecurity, and anxiety.

Women who have these timelines believe in them. They trust them to help make sound decisions. Now there is a conflict between the timeline and the perception of time.

It has been said that men don't commit at the right time, they commit to the right woman. The time distortion from online communications can make us feel we have found the right woman very quickly.

Whether or not we are right in that idea is far less important than keeping it to ourselves until the woman can get her sense of timeline back on track.

If we jump the gun because of the perception distortion, it can wreck the relationship. It may very well scare her off. Take a breath and remind yourself that the feeling of time is not the reality of time. If she is the right woman, waiting will be worth it.

It's best for everyone to just relax and enjoy the process of getting to know each other. Be aware of the time distortion, but don't let it impact you.

If you are writing a story of any kind, remember that inserting connection disruptions can help build the connection between the audience and your characters.

When you are texting, remember that you are like a movie editor, building up the perception of time with each other with every message. This isn't good or bad. It just is the reality. Accept it and notice it.

I bet you're going to watch the opening of Star Wars now.

Friend Zone Roolz

"Let's just be friends."

Nobody wants to these words smacking into their eardrums. It's gut wrenching, always disappointing, maybe even devastating, depending on the depth of the relationship to that point.

That sentence means:

A. She likes you but doesn't want to date you.
B. She doesn't like you and wants to get away without a fuss. She will not be friends.

(Yes, I'm taking the position that the woman is the one who wants to be friends. Mentally flip it around if it bothers you. I'm not going to spend half my word count on disclaimers. Live with it.)

B is simple. She will ghost the minute she is out of sight. It's the last you will hear from her.

A is the problem, the challenge, the path strewn with land mines. Women have no idea what it takes for a man to agree to being friends with a woman in whom he has (or had) a romantic/sexual interest. Let's fix that.

What does it mean to be friends with a woman? It means certain activities/behaviors are now out-of-bounds, off-limits. No flirting. No kissing. No touching.

That is significant because a smart man knows there is almost no chance of escaping the friend zone without those chemistry-building actions. Yet, that's what it means to be just friends. *Friends don't kiss.* Every day the chances of getting out of the zone diminishes because he can't work on the chemistry.

Personally, I believe respecting the boundaries of friendship mean not try to change them. It's up to her to let me know if she changes her mind.

For the Women

The thing is, ladies, the man wants you, wants to be with you, wants to have sex with you. As your friend, he doesn't get to show this side.

Doesn't mean it goes away, though.

The man will act as if he doesn't have those feelings anymore because that's how a gentleman behaves with a woman who is a friend. He respects the boundaries. He protects her feelings. He swallows his hurt, buries his desires, so she can feel safe and comfortable with him.

Respect this effort, then. Don't make him your girlfriend and take him shopping or gossip endlessly. Don't parade around in skimpy outfits or underwear. Don't be a tease, and do not ever flirt. He doesn't want to know about your dates. Don't talk about sex or your boobs, and please, do nothing that could be mistaken for you changing your mind.

If a man wants you but knows he can't have you and yet still wants to be around you, that is a significant sacrifice on his part, and it says a lot about what he thinks of you. Don't squander the opportunity.

Just because he acts like he no longer has an interest in you does not mean he has no more interest in you. He's just not allowed to let you see that aspect of himself. Keeping the lid on passions can be very difficult.

If you do change your mind, be very clear, direct, and unambiguous. No [very long list of profanity] hints. That is an excellent rule for any interaction with a man, by the way.

For the Men

If you want to avoid the friend zone, there are a few things to remember.

Women think differently about finding a partner. While we look for reasons to include a woman in our search, women tend to look for reasons to exclude men. Mostly, they aren't even aware they do this.

Seemingly innocent, get-to-know-you questions are their way of trying to find out if you should be excluded. Anything you say or do can, and will, be used against you. Be careful out there.

The best way to stay out of the zone is to kiss her, because *friends don't kiss*. Wait for the right moment, lean in slowly, and then… read the chapter "Fucking Kiss Her Like a Man."

Sometimes, we still get invited to the zone in spite of our best efforts. Follow these tips to make the best of the situation.

- Say no to the friend request if you aren't certain you can keep the lid on how you feel. Sometimes the passion runs too strong. In that case, it's better for everybody to make a clean break.

- If you decide to go the friend route, do so with open eyes. You will almost certainly never escape the zone. Respect the boundaries. Never push them, never complain about them.
- Set your own boundaries with her and enforce the rules with her. It will be a little bit easier to keep on your side of the line. It also shows you're not a wimp.

Cheating Cheaters Who Cheat

Have you ever cheated on your partner?

You could respond in one of a very few ways but it only gets interesting when you can get past the knee-jerk yes or no answers because there is one very important piece of information that you are assuming and I bet my dirty underpants in the hamper you don't know what it is. [*That's a bet you don't want to win.* – Editor]

You are holding tight to the assumption that we agree on the definition of cheating. In fact, a great many of you think there is but One Definition to Rule Them All. And that everybody subscribes to that definition.

This will come as a surprise to you but – are you sitting down? – there isn't a single common definition of cheating.

Whoa. Ka-boom. Mind *BLOWN*.

I used to be part of the crowd subscribing to the Broadly Accepted Rules of Fidelity (BARF), and proud member of the Never Cheated club. [*Membership is small and dwindling.* – SK]

While still a member of the club, life has taught me the BARF is a myth. Religions have their hard-and-fast rules of fidelity, and then they have their guidelines, and finally the suggestions. The ordering of these varies from religion to religion.

The religious influence on the concept of fidelity run so deep, even atheists often hold to the religious definitions.

The origins of fidelity trace back to the earliest days of church/state sanctioned marriage, which was invented to enable the creation of family alliances. Women became property to be traded. Children were owned by the husband until they became husbands themselves or were traded to other men.

Cheating (on the part of the women) had to be condemned or the alliances would fail. The man needed some level of assurance the woman's offspring were his because frankly he had to rely on her word. [*Thankfully, we have DNA testing now.* – SK]

This still goes on in some societies, and to a lesser extent, in some classes in Western cultures. Happily, for the rest of us, we are no longer beholden to these barbaric rites and customs.

Now, if we don't have the BARF to tell us what is cheating and what isn't, how do we answer the question? At some point, this is a question that can move instantly from theoretical to the concrete in a nanosecond. Better know how to respond before the question comes up.

Let me humbly suggest a definition that will work for everyone.

Cheating is what you and your partner decide it is.

Seriously, nobody else has a fucking say in the matter. Just you two (or three, or however many). You are the ones who know what you want, what you like, what your aims and ambitions are for your relationship, and what the deal breakers are.

You get to decide this shit for yourselves and fuck everyone else. (Unless that's part of your agreement. Not judging.)

If you are following the Roolz that everyone involved has *explicitly* agreed to then you aren't cheating.

If you decide that the agreed-upon Roolz no longer work for you then you need to renegotiate them. With the understanding that your partner(s) may not agree to the changes. That's the risk you take. That's the risk everyone takes.

Give the goddamn guilt back to the preachers and decide what makes you happy and then stick with that.

How to Fucking Talk to Men

Raise your hands if you are adult human females who interact with the male of the species. You are the ones I'm going to talk to for a minute. Raise your other hand if you have ever worried about being thought of as a nag.

I'm going to give you some very simple instructions for how to get a man to do things for you without nagging.

(Put your hands down now. I can't believe you really raised them.)

Perhaps you notice there are differences between men and women? No, I'm serious. Despite modern equality advances, and shifting roles and responsibilities, fundamental genetic differences remain. Evolution can't rewrite those in just a few decades.

Here's one that is key to getting a man to do things.

Men are hardwired to provide for those they care about. They need to do this. They must do this, just like you need to build the finest nest (home) you can.

But it is a yuuuge mistake to think of providing only in terms of income. Men can provide in countless ways.

One of the other ways men's and women's brains function differently: men have single-focus attention while women have what's called 'diffuse awareness'—which is why when you walk into a messy room you notice All The Things, and they all are screaming at you, and they are all equally important.

When a man enters a room, it's for a purpose and unless the purpose is to clean the room the state of the room is not a factor in his thinking. [*OCD changes everything, however.* – Editor]

OK, here is your magic no-more-nagging formula. Which is hilarious because men are always looking for a magic formula for women but there aren't any.

Do not interrupt him while he is engrossed. Remember single focus? Work with that, not against it. Find a time when he is not deeply engaged with something then say, "I have something to ask of you. When would be a good time to talk about it?"

For the love of god, do not *ever* say, "We need to talk" unless you follow up with "—about" and even then, it's a bad idea. Those four words put men into a panic. Look at their faces when you say those words. See that pain, that fear? Is that what you want in a relationship?

When the time comes to ask for, say, taking out the garbage in a timely manner, talk to him in terms of what it will provide for you. Tell him why it is important to you and how much it will mean to you if he does it. This kind of talk will trigger the provider in him to action.

He doesn't just know these things because you do. He views the garbage in a completely different way from you, and it is damn annoying that you expect him to think the way you do. Allow his differences and work with them, not against them.

Let's say he has seen the light and now understands why the piled-up garbage matters to you. It would be a mistake to jump in and give him a schedule and instructions, and act like he is incapable of doing the task. That will simply guarantee he will not do the job.

If he asks for suggestions or ideas, fine. But do not offer them unsolicited.

One final step and this may be the most challenging part of all.

Let him do it his way, in his time.

Unless you want the job back, in which case just shut up about it in the first place.

If you tell him how he did it wrong, if you remind him, if you say anything other than thank you, you wasted your time and made matters even worse.

While on the subject of asking, next time you catch yourself thinking, or saying, "Why would he do that?" there is a very simple step you can take to turn a rhetorical presupposition into information.

"I'm sure you had a very good reason for doing/saying what you did. Would you mind telling me what it was?" And, again, very important to shut up until he finishes. You will learn a great deal.

Go ahead and put this to the test. Let me know how it goes.

Part V: The Tools

You Fucking Need Help

Look. I get it.

I was a total dick when it came to the idea of therapy. I actually scoffed, and that's just not done these days. I had to look up how to do it.

Why, I asked myself, would I pay to talk to someone? I can talk to people for free. And they might even give good advice from time to time, which seemed to put random people ahead of the professionals.

Besides, how effective can it be if people keep going for decades and show little improvement? Fucking con artists.

Do you know how stupid that was? It was like saying I don't believe in socket wrenches.

Men love the adage of the right tool for the job, but mostly while they are at Home Depot trying to justify a new power miter saw. When it comes to the slush between their ears, not so much.

Women are more likely to seek out professional help, but that's not a hard-won trophy. Don't brag so much about it. Besides, just because you go doesn't mean you are getting anywhere. Plenty of women are seeing someone who will justify the shit they do to their partners, friends, and kids.

I needed to become lost in the wilderness, so to speak, before realizing I could not go it alone anymore. I had to reach a point where I had no clue where to go or how to get there. I had to find a professional, soon.

Which presents another dilemma.

Everyone knows at least one person who has struggled to find a good fit with a therapist. They try one, seems ok at first, but then things go to shit and within six months they are on the hunt again. They go through referrals like it was Tinder for Neurotics.

[What would that app be called? Splinter? Tender? Bender? No, that would be for AA people. – SK]

What the fuck are these people doing? How are they going about selecting one of the most important professional relationships they will ever have? Casting bones? Studying chicken blood splatters? Waiting for their dead grandma to whisper it to them in their sleep?

This shit is important. Far too important to wing it, to hope this time the person will be good. You gotta have a fucking plan.

I'm telling you, if you're reading this book, then you are probably fucked up enough to need professional help. That's not a slam. Not entirely. The whole world is fucked up. The difference is you seem to be a person who just might, maybe, someday, decide to become a little bit less fucked up.

How do you find a good therapist? To begin with, define "good" in this case. I'm sorry, but this does mean you will need to think a little bit.

Morons want a doctor who will back their play after the fact. Who will just nod and say what a good little boy or girl you are, that none of it is your fault. It's all those big mean people out there.

What the fuck do you want from therapy? You might as well start thinking about it because the doc is going to ask you on the first day.

For the love of god, no, wanting to feel better is not a valid answer. Thanks for playing.

Feeling better is an outcome. It's the result of making well-targeted changes.

What kind of person are you hoping to become, and what is keeping you from being that person today?

Those are better questions.

Now, what kind of therapist specializes in the things that are holding you back? Was it trauma? Of course, it was fucking trauma. Jesus. Everybody has been through trauma.

So maybe don't look at the relationship specialists, ok? Even if you think their profile photo is hot.

Especially.

There are a few more filters to apply. Geography is an obvious one. Insurance coverage. Sex is another. Age range. Pretty soon the overwhelming number of possibilities is down to a manageable size.

What do sex and age have to do with the quality of therapy? Maybe nothing directly. They do factor into one's comfort level. Personally, I wanted a female doctor with plenty of experience, but not yet a leather-faced schoolmistress with bony fingers snapping at you. Maybe that's just me. And not so good looking that it would make me uncomfortable talking about potentially embarrassing topics. Like girls.

For me, I wanted a trauma specialist trained in Eye Movement Desensitization and Reprocessing (EMDR – see Resources for a link). I wanted a woman doctor who was middle-aged and not distractingly attractive.

Yes, there were hot young women doctors, but I wasn't looking for a fucking date. I had a shitload of work to do, and I was in one motherfucker of a hurry.

That's how I found Doc Awesome on the first try. We've been seeing each other for nearly five years now. It's a tremendous relationship that saw me through incredible amounts of growth in a matter of months.

Part of that is because of how I used Doc Awesome.

Imagine your neighbor's car breaks down. She's a handy woman who likes a challenge, so she goes to the hardware and auto parts stores and buys all the shit she needs to fix her car.

She comes home and lays the tools out next to the car and goes inside to watch TV.

Every day, she goes out to see if the car has been fixed. Of course, it hasn't. This goes on for a month until she becomes so mad she throws the tools away and goes to a different hardware store and buys new ones.

This completely stupid allegory is how most people do therapy.

They bring their broken asses into the office and sit with the best tools for the job and expect the tools to do all the goddamn work. It doesn't fucking work that way.

The doctor is your toolbox. But like a smart toolbox that you can ask questions.

Believe me, your doctor will be happy to take your money while you cry on the sofa. But just maybe you might want to, you know, get some shit done while you're both there.

Tell the doctor what the fuck you want to accomplish. And for the last time, it isn't to feel better. Jesus. Pay attention.

Ask the doctor for ideas on how to get the shit done that you need help with. Hell, come prepared with some thoughts on that. If you want to do EMDR, say so. If you don't want to do EMDR, then you're an idiot who deserves to suffer.

Kick around the idea of medications. Discuss the options and drawbacks and which dealers have the best prices.

If your doc gives you an assignment, then do the damn assignment. Almost like a grown-up.

If you (and your insurance) can handle it, consider visiting more than once a week. I found this of enormous benefit for the first two years.

One last thing about this part. Get used to the idea that you're seeing a therapist. Get used to telling people. I don't mean starting a conversation on the bus with, "I'm in therapy."

The stigma just ain't there like it used to be. If you're in the dating world (god help you) being in therapy is a good sign, and probably more necessary than ever. Also, you look like a person who is working on their shit. It's attractive.

What if you can't afford regular therapy? Then of course you are justified remaining stuck in your neuroses. It's not your fault, you can't do anything about them.

ROFLMFAO

Go hide under your bed and wait for mommy to make it all better. Or get off your ass and find some goddamn options. For fuck's sake, stand on your hind legs and take charge of your fucking miserable life.

The interwebs be chock full of information. Why haven't you done this yet?

Just bear in mind that if you are going to use a placebo method— I mean something woo-woo—that it's ok, *if* it gets the job done.

Be pragmatic about this shit. Either something works for you, or it doesn't. That's the only measure that counts. If you get better, if you lose some of your baggage, if you lose your anxieties, and that kind of shit. Not just feeling better.

Getting wasted feels better, but it doesn't fix shit.

Do the world a favor and get some fucking help.

P.S. I was just in the kitchen warming some soup and thinking about the first time my book is brought up in a therapy session.

"Interesting you should mention that. I was reading The Little Book of Big Roolz the other day—"

"Reading whaaat?"

"The Little Book of Big Roolz, except rules is spelled r-o-o-l-z, and he said—"

"Why is it spelled like that?"

"I don't know, actually. Trying to be funny, I suppose."

"Is it a comic book?"

"No. It's a—"

"It sounds like a children's book."

"It's not. I don't know how to describe it. Anyway, he said—"

"Who said?"

"SK."

"Who is SK?"

"Oh my god. He said this would happen."

And then they read the part of the book describing the therapy session word-for-word, causing the entire universe to collapse in on itself.

The Struggle Is Real

Get busy living or get busy dying. – Andy Dufresne, *Shawshank Redemption*

Most people are alive by accident.

No, I don't mean the condom broke. I mean, they were born and then they remain alive (to the extent they do) out of habit.

A few people attempt to end their own lives, botch it, and then go on to be alive deliberately. One of my brothers went through that, but it's a fucking risky highway and not at all recommended.

The rest of the world, with rare exception, are alive because they don't kill themselves and not because they want to live.

People talk all the fucking time about wanting to live a different/better life, but they haven't taken the needed prerequisite courses.

1. They have not consciously chosen to be alive, and to do their damnedest to stay that way.
2. Having decided to live, they still need to decide to *live*.

Don't fucking pretend you don't know what I mean. You know the ones (just like you) who cruise through existence checking boxes and lists, waiting for the fucking reaper to tap them on the shoulder.

They (you) don't decide to *live* any more than they (you) choose to be alive. Most of what you do was decided by other people when you were still licking snot from your upper lip.

And you just went along with it once you cleared puberty. Name one fucking time you bucked the system as an adult and chose to live differently. Maybe you have one. How about more than one?

Are you thrilled with your fucked-up, shitty existence? Of course not. Your dissatisfaction relates directly to the degree you waved the white flag to please others. Nothing will fucking change until you decide those two things above: to stay alive, and to fucking **live** as hard, well, and amazingly, and long as you are allotted.

There is power in deciding, even when it scares the pee out of you. You cannot mope around once you have chosen life and chosen to live it for real. There is energy, vitality, in those decisions.

Humans are organisms like any other, and like all other organisms, we are either growing or we are dying.

What's it going to be?

But....

I know what you're thinking because I've been there a bazillion times already.

"I've tried making different choices. Tried everything under the sun, and nothing works for long."

Yup. That's why How-To books really are What-To books. None of them tell you how the fuck to do what they say to do.

I wouldn't do that to you, leave you hanging like that.

SK's Fractal Theory of Life

According to The Fractal Foundation, "A fractal is a never-ending pattern. Fractals are infinitely complex patterns that are self-similar across different scales." Meaning, the patterns are the same at a small scale and at a large scale. For example, a Douglas Fir tree has needles that are roughly the same shape as the whole tree. For another example, a jagged mountain is made up of jagged rocks and not round river rocks.

So, what the fuck does this have to do with life choices?

Everyone's life is fractal at the decision level, meaning the big choices are made up of a lot of smaller choices that look similar. A person doesn't wake up one morning and decide out of the blue to rob a bank instead of going to work. Lots of similar-looking decisions preceded that one big choice.

If you want to make better large-scale choices, then you have to change the shape of the thousands of tiny decisions that fill each day. The challenge is that we are largely unaware of most of these. They happen so quickly we only notice them, if at all, after the fact.

The best way to become aware is to simply start paying attention. I don't know any other way. Sorry.

Altering States

The woman had a clean, simple beauty. Iceberg eyes, silver-blonde hair, lean, strong. She worked at Trader Joe's. Worked hard, the times I saw her.

I had yet to ask a woman out as a newly minted single man. Decided she would be the first. The objective was the asking. If she accepted that would be a bonus.

Walked into the store and immediately spotted her. My heart pounded harder with each step. And then I veered off into the dairy section. *Whew! That was close!*

Trying to act like a casual shopper, I tossed a few random items into my little red basket while slowly looping back around to where the woman was working. The closer I got, the more anxious I became until *vvvrrrrooooommm*, I was off to frozen foods.

It was during the fourth or fifth lap of the store that I became aware of my internal dialog, wherein I was fucking talking myself *out* of asking her. As long as I was telling myself all the goddamn reasons why not to ask her, it would be impossible to go through with it.

We do this shit to ourselves all the time. You know what I'm talking about. We try to do the right thing (or avoid doing the wrong thing) but when it gets right to it, we change our internal dialog and talk ourselves out of it. Then we feel like dog shit for failing.

The more tired we get, the worse this becomes, too. Then the voices just have to say, "I'm too tired, fuck this shit." And we are all like, hellz yeah, fuck this shit. Because tired!

Here's the trick I learned wearing out the floor at Trader Joe's: you can change that internal dialog. And it is stupid simple. (What's harder is to fucking *remember* to do it.)

When you hear/feel that internal struggle, stop for a second, and instead of whatever version of no you are saying to yourself, just replace it with yes. That's it, the whole enchilada.

The dirty glass that's been sitting on the dresser for three days? (To give an entirely fictional and not-at-all realistic example.) When your brain says *no* to moving it to the dishwasher, stop and say *yes*. And keep replacing no with yes until the brain gives up and lets you deal with the glass.

The great thing about this technique is that it doesn't fucking matter *why* I—er, you—left the glass there for three days. It doesn't matter if you were given PTSD by Mickey Mouse as a kid. It only matters what you are saying to yourself right the fuck now.

Well, yes, of course, it works the other way around. Duh.

This is how I finally managed to ask the woman out for coffee. It was a nice little conversation and she was sweet as hell. She said no, but as I said before, getting her to agree wasn't the goal. Asking was the goal.

Choosing to remain alive. Choosing to live the best life you can. These are within your grasp once you decide, and now you have a way to turn those decisions whatever direction you want.

The fight isn't with the doing of a thing, it's with the deciding.

Getting Self Worth Is So Easy You Won't Do It

Worth! Huh!
What is it good for?
Absolutely something!

Sometimes I forget the kiddies among the readers have only been alive about two minutes and won't get the lyrical reference that I spoofed above. But too bad. Us old bastards will get it.

Right?

The question is valid, though. What the hell good is self-worth? Why does it even matter?

A decade ago, I was in a screenwriting program. One of instructors posited (that means he offered a fucking theory) that writers keep revisiting their deepest issues over and over in their scripts, trying to resolve them through their characters.

As we worked through some exercises designed to elicit our own deepest shit, a pattern emerged. Although not universal, even in a class of 30, most of the students came up with this.

Am I lovable?

This question drives a huge fraction of the human population. And the amount of suckage attached to this even being a question is beyond measure. So much pain, suffering, wreckage, and really bad relationship choices can be traced back to this question.

It ought not to even exist.

But people are fucked up and almost all of them pass on their fucked-upedness to others, especially their children. Not just the kids, but they get it the worst.

What the question is actually asking is, "Am I worth loving?"

There are people out wandering loose who have never held a doubt about this. They had parents who loved them completely and showed their love in all they did, and they expressed their love for their children in many ways, including with words.

I have so much respect and appreciation for such parents that I can't even do justice to them with words except to say thank you for being good parents. You are in the minority.

What Is So Fucking Unlovable?

We do not have the ability to see ourselves as the world sees us. We know all the shit we have going on inside our heads. We know our faults, our flaws, our weaknesses, all of which we work so goddamn hard to hide.

We are ashamed of these things. We want others to see us as we wish we were. I mean, you do. Not me. Nope. Well, perhaps once upon a time. But not anymore! [*Sure thing.* – Editor]

People around us growing up (and often later in life, too, the bastards) convinced us that our (countless) imperfections are shameful, that other people do not suffer from such horrible flaws. Just look at them. Those people do everything just right. Why can't you be more like them?

It's a very short walk from feeling ashamed of ourselves to believing nobody could possibly love us if they saw our faults.

Uh oh!

Guess what? They already do see our flaws. No matter how much we work to keep them buried, they can't help but emerge eventually. And yet we persist in the notion that we are only lovable to the extent we can hide our true selves from the world, and most especially from our romantic partners.

Our experience has taught us that being truly seen as we are is a source of pain and rejection. As we learned in Why Making Changes Feels Like Dying, our biological wiring tells us that rejection means literal death.

We reach the completely reasonable conclusion that to be loved and avoid rejection, we must not have any flaws. Not any noticeable flaws, at least. But we know that we have a metric shit ton of faults. Ergo, we aren't lovable.

That's a nasty little bastard of a Catch-22.

Now What?

If you don't know who Brené Brown is, stop right the fuck now and look up her TED talks (see Resources). Go now. I mean it because she says too much too well, and I'm not about to take a hatchet to her words and ideas to provide a shitty summary.

If you desire to live as your true self, to live with courage and compassion, and to come to believe you are worthy of love, then you must love yourself completely. Especially your flaws.

Yes, that makes you vulnerable. That is the point. Your flaws are what make you uniquely you, and the combination of your skills, talents, abilities, desires, plus your flaws, are what make you beautiful.

Listen to her. She explains it better than I ever could.

There is a way to love yourself that much. But it's too easy, and you won't do it.

Collecting the Pieces

Valori

It had been a very long time since last I was a single man, and what little skill I may have had around dating had no present value. As a newly single man, I wanted to meet women, I wanted to love again, and I had no idea where to begin. I was frankly a little bit terrified. Just a little.

I went to one of my goodest friends, Valori, for advice.

She said, "Honestly, the best way to attract a woman is to just be yourself."

I laughed out loud and slapped the arm of the sofa. "Why would I ever do that?"

To me, the idea was both ridiculous and impossible. There was no way a woman I might be interested in would want to see the real me. It wasn't even debatable. I thought it was a rhetorical question but Valori had a ready answer.

"Because someone out there is looking for exactly who you are. If you hide any part of yourself, she won't recognize you. But," she warned, "you have to love yourself before you can do that."

Oh, fuck. It was worse than I thought.

Doc Awesome

Months later when I walked into my regular session, Doc Awesome greeted me with her usual, "How are you doing today?"

"Pretty good," I said. "Of course, when I feel good, I'm more likely to take proper care of myself." It was a simple observation, and common enough, I felt sure. Just a little pre-session chit-chat.

What she said in response changed my world, not for the first or last time. She said,

When we take care of ourselves, especially when we don't feel like it, we prove our own worth to ourselves.

This stuff is why I call her Doc Awesome.

Proving my worth. To me. Not just saying I have worth, but proving it, day after day. The idea churned in my brain, ricocheting off other bits of stored knowledge until a light bulb exploded in my head.

The Experiment

The reason affirmations don't work, or if they do it takes fucking forever, is because the unconscious mind requires proof. Evidence. It won't just take our word that we are worthy or lovable, or whatever attribute we want to change.

If I say to the mirror, "I am a successful, rich, confident man" my unconscious mind says, "I see nothing to back up such a claim. Nothing in the database supports it. Request for belief change denied."

How could I turn flossing my teeth into proving my worth to myself? By matching the words with evidence.

I stood at the sink and said out loud, "I am worth flossing my teeth." And then I did it. The brain heard the words and then got the proof immediately.

"I am worth making the bed." Then I made the bed.

"I am worth going for a walk." Then I went for a walk.

All day long, whenever I did something good for myself, I turned it into proof of my own worth. It was exhilarating. Energy surged throughout my body. It was exciting, it was working, and faster than I could possibly imagine. Those gooey lumps in our skulls are pretty quick on the uptake.

Confirmation

After a week of this barrage of proof, I was talking on the phone with my oldest niece. She said, "You sound different. What's going on?"

"I am different. It's hard to explain exactly what this feels like," I said, struggling to name all the great emotions swirling around inside of me, but there was something familiar about this cocktail. And when it hit me, it took my breath away.

"It feels like being in love. I love...me."

Finally. And then I cried, for joy, for no longer having to struggle through life without this essential element, for gratitude at finding a path to this moment when so many never do.

I went to see Valori the next day.

I had barely stepped inside the apartment when she said, "You've changed." She studied my face. "I like this guy much better."

It Really Is That Simple

Please, do not fucking take my word for it. Do not believe me.

There is no fucking reason on this goddamn earth why you should believe me. I don't have credentials, I don't have peer-reviewed research papers. I'm just a guy who put the right pieces together, who connected dots that have been well-known in certain circles for a long time.

Find out for yourself. What's the downside if it doesn't work? Nothing!

Most of you won't even bother. It's too fucking simple. People spend years, decades, in therapy of every imaginable kind trying to sort out this shit. They take drugs of every sort, hoping to feel better about themselves. Even the hard shit doesn't work this fast.

Why would some idiot smartass figure out the world's fastest shortcut to self-worth? I have no idea why. And frankly, it doesn't matter. It happened. Get over it.

But, since you took the time to read this chapter, you now have zero excuses for walking around without loving yourself.

Either do it and reap the benefits, or shut the fuck up about your shitty self-worth. But you know what will happen if you don't.

One day you will meet someone who did bother, who did do it, and they will glow, literally glow, with love for themselves, and they will begin to tell you about how it happened. It will sound familiar. Then you will realize it was this stupid fucking chapter they are talking about.

And you will suddenly regret your skepticism and the time you wasted living without self-worth because you were too fucking smart to try it. You'll be too embarrassed to admit you read this and never did it.

Don't be the person with regrets. Be the glowy person.

Open Doors

Walk through the doors that open for you. – Dr. Robert Glover

In the waning days of 2014, I was listening to a podcast by Dr. Robert Glover, author of *No More Mr. Nice Guy*. He closed with the above quote. Eight fucking words that changed the course of my life.

You know, if you keep your head in the sand, or up your ass, nothing in your life is going to get better. But if you become a seeker of answers with an open mind and you embrace serendipity then amazing things begin to happen. And those things lead to other great things, and wonders will unfold like a room full of tumbling dominoes.

When I replay the sequence of events in my life backwards, tracing the cause and effect of one moment on another, it becomes difficult to speak. I get choked up with amazement and awe that such things should befall me, of all people.

Somehow, I managed to listen to the words and not let them bounce off my forehead. Upon reflection, I realized I had too often been afraid to walk through open doors. So, I decided to change that. I would look for doors to walk through.

Didn't take long at all to find one. In fact, it had presented itself a few days earlier. My inbox contained an invitation to a writer's retreat in January 2015 I had mentally brushed aside as not my thing.

It felt like a really bad idea to spend a long weekend at the ocean with a bunch of writers, where I only knew one person. I was not able to call myself a writer. Instead, I said I liked to write. Being a writer was a label that didn't fit. Sharing my humble words with actual writers intimidated the shit out of me.

But I wasn't going to let myself off the hook so easily. I accepted the invitation. And I actually showed up.

Christ, is there a limit to the number of life-changing events one man is allowed? Because I can list them all fucking day. And I don't ever want them to stop happening.

At the retreat, I met Jackie, an incredible woman who ran a literary site and events. She asked me to submit some words for publication. A week later, I wrote a horror story for an anthology of sorts, and it was accepted. My first publication evaaaar.

At the launch party, I met Lisa, one of the other contributors. We seemed to click, at least on the smartass level.

Lisa and I went on a non-date date to one of those wine and painting events, where we followed step-by-step instructions to paint some sunflowers. In an unexpected twist, doing the painting tapped something in me I didn't know was there. A need, a hunger, to create more art.

A couple of days later, I was wandering the aisles of an art supply store looking for ideas of what medium my art would follow. Out of the corner of my eye, just barely, I saw the cover of a book that stopped me dead in my tracks.

I had found my style right there on the shelf. The digits you see with the section breaks are some of the work I've created since then.

Jackie published a few more stories, and I spoke at her readings a few times.

Which led to being invited to write a monthly column for a startup online magazine. Which scared the shit out of me, but I knew the experience would be important. I wrote some of the most-read articles and blog posts for the magazine.

You get the idea.

Follow the dominoes a bit longer and suddenly here you are reading words I wrote for you. All because of those eight words.

It seems like there might be a downside to this. Maybe there is, but I haven't run across it. Perhaps it's a matter of applying some instincts and judgment to avoid actual perils.

Doors open when we are on the move already. Nobody runs an open door delivery service, you lazy fuckers! Start taking steps, trying new shit, and looking for new experiences, meeting new people.

It is all about the people, in the end. The best ones are beyond the open doors.

Fucking Practice

OK, look, I'm trying my best to stop writing more shit and get the book out the door, but this one is too important to leave out.

People are dumb shits who know a lot more than they do. People generalize the wrong shit.

Everyone knows the way to improve a skill is to practice. When was the last time you practiced anything? High school? The first week on a new job?

We know about practicing sports and music and theater. Those we get, and for some stupid fucking reason we think practice only applies to those areas. What kind of dumb shit thinking is that?

You had to practice walking. Talking. Social skills. Writing. Literally everything you know how to do is a thing you had to practice doing.

So why did you stop?

For fuck's sake, we gripe about how bad we are at day-to-day shit, and yet it never even *occurs* to us to fucking practice that shit.

Want to be better at getting up in the morning? Practice that shit the night before. Seriously. Set up your room and get ready for bed. Set the clock ahead to five minutes before your alarm. Turn off the lights and pretend to sleep. When the alarm goes off, run through your new morning routine. Then do it all again. And again.

Want to be better at going to the gym? Start by practicing getting ready. Just that part. When you get comfortable with that, add in driving to the gym. Just drive there and park for a minute. After that gets easier, just go inside and walk around the floor. See how I'm breaking it down into steps? That's how you practice life. Baby steps.

Want to be better at listening to other people? (Hey, you, I'm talking to you.) Practice that shit.

There is literally no skill that you can't improve at through dedicated practice. Even the mundane shit we love to brag about being terrible at.

We don't practice the ordinary shit because it never occurred to us that those are practicable skills. Well, ain't we the dumb shits, then. But we don't have to be.

Now we know we can practice and get better at life.

How to Be Funny

Don't.

Part VI: Postscript

Resources

Books

Ruiz, Don Miguel et al. The Four Agreements. San Rafael: Amber-Allen Publishing, 2001. Print.

Colvin, Geoff. Talent Is Overrated. New York: Portfolio, 2008. Print.

Coyle, Daniel. The Talent Code. New York: Bantam, 2009. Print.

Gladwell, Malcolm. Blink. New York: Little, Brown and Company, 2005. Print.

EMDR

http://www.emdr.com/what-is-emdr/

TED Talks
Visit www.ted.com to view:

Why You Think You're Right
https://www.ted.com/talks/julia_galef_why_you_think_you_re_right_even_if_you_re_wrong

Body Language
http://www.ted.com/talks/amy_cuddy_your_body_language_shapes_who_you_are

On Being Wrong
http://www.ted.com/talks/kathryn_schulz_on_being_wrong

Bréne Brown on Vulnerability
https://www.ted.com/talks/brene_brown_on_vulnerability?language=en

Bibliography

Marshall, Sebastian. Ikigai. The One Week Book, 2011. Kindle.

Miller, Alice. The Drama of the Gifted Child. New York: Basic Books, 2008. Print.

Gonzales, Laurence. Deep Survival. New York: W. W. Norton & Company, 2003. Print.

Armstrong, Alison. The Queen's Code. Glendora: PAX Programs Incorporated, 2013. Print.

Glover, Robert. No More Mr. Nice Guy. New York: Running Press Adult, 2003. Print.

Additional References

Jussim, Lee. "Truth in Stereotypes". https://aeon.co/essays/truth-lies-and-stereotypes-when-scientists-ignore-evidence

The End

Jeezus, what more do you want? That's all there is. It's over.

Go away, until the next book comes out.

About the Author

SK Berit is a writer of fiction, non-fiction, creative non-fiction, semi-fiction, and quasi-fiction. Pretty much anything with the word fiction in it. He dabbles in photography and animal cloning. In 2003, he was the recipient of the prestigious H.M.L. Blakely Award [not a real thing – Editor] for his screenplay "Zunderberger" based on the secret underground Nazi bases in Greenland built for musical theater development. Proceeds from the award allowed him to spend the next several years researching the origins of the idiom "believe you me" and trying to strike that delicate balance between dumbass and smartass.

Social Media

Facebook: www.facebook.com/skberitauthor
Twitter: @skberit
Instagram: @skberitofficial
Web site: skberit.com

Coming Soon

'Soon' is a relative concept. For example, as I slump against the desk, desperately hoping against hope that this book might come to a fucking end, saying that book two is coming soon fills me with impending doom.

By the time you read this, it might very well be imminent. Or even available already.

In fact, when viewed at a historical scale, much more time will pass after the above volume has been published than now exists between the first and second editions.

Let's not even start on light speed.

Fucking time, man. Fucking time.

Made in the USA
Columbia, SC
23 June 2019